How to *Succeed* as a Freelancer in Publishing

Visit our How To website at www.howto.co.uk

At www.howto.co.uk you can engage in conversation with our authors – all of whom have 'been there and done that' in their specialist fields. You can get access to special offers and additional content but most importantly you will be able to engage with, and become a part of, a wide and growing community of people just like yourself.

At www.howto.co.uk you'll be able to talk and share tips with people who have similar interests and are facing similar challenges in their lives. People who, just like you, have the desire to change their lives for the better – be it through moving to a new country, starting a new business, growing their own vegetables, or writing a novel.

At www.howto.co.uk you'll find the support and encouragement you need to help make your aspirations a reality.

You can go direct to www.how-to-succeed-as-a-freelancer-in-publishing.co.uk which is part of the main How To site.

How To Books strives to present authentic, inspiring, practical information in their books. Now, when you buy a title from How To Books, you get even more than just words on a page.

How to *Succeed* as a Freelancer in Publishing

THE COMPLETE GUIDE

EMMA MURRAY & CHARLIE WILSON

howtobooks

Published by How To Books Ltd,
Spring Hill House, Spring Hill Road,
Begbroke, Oxford OX5 1RX, United Kingdom
Tel: (01865) 375794 Fax: (01865) 379162
info@howtobooks.co.uk
www.howtobooks.co.uk

How To Books greatly reduce the carbon footprint of their books by sourcing their typesetting and printing in the UK.

British Library Cataloguing in Publication Data.
A catalogue record for this book is available from the British Library.

ISBN 978 1 84528 423 7

Produced for How To Books by Deer Park Productions, Tavistock
Typeset by PDQ Typesetting, Newcastle-under-Lyme, Staffordshire
Printed and bound in Great Britain by Bell & Bain Ltd, Glasgow

NOTE: The material contained in this book is set out in good faith for general guidance and no liability can be accepted for loss or expense incurred as a result of relying in particular circumstances on statements made in the book. Laws and regulations are complex and liable to change, and readers should check the current position with the relevant authorities before making personal arrangements.

CONTENTS

ACKNOWLEDGEMENTS

Being a freelancer is all about having faith and confidence in your own abilities. But in order to believe in yourself, you also need support from the people around you. Luckily, between the two of us, we have managed to generate a large network of contacts in the publishing world that have offered both advice and unending support through the good times and the bad, some of whom have been featured in this book.

On that note, we would like to thank all the contributors to this book who took the time and effort to share their own experiences and realities from the world of publishing. This book is all the better for their words of wisdom and inspirational stories, and we hope they will help you on your journey towards becoming a successful freelancer.

Finally, we would also like to thank our long-suffering husbands for talking us down off the freelance cliff of uncertainty during the difficult times, and celebrating with us during those joyous times when things really did take off! Sam and Ally, we salute you!

INTRODUCTION

Working on what you want, when you want. Determining your own salary, and setting your own goals. Sleeping late, and taking holidays when you fancy. Ah, freelancing...

But hang on, what about finding clients? How much do you charge? How do you market yourself? How do you decide which services to offer? What on earth are you supposed to do with a tax return?!

Welcome to the world of freelancing. It's a career choice that ultimately brings you freedom, flexibility, challenge and many opportunities for development, but there's a lot to learn along the way. And sometimes all the stuff you have to contend with in running your freelancing business can be pretty daunting and stressful – especially when it seems there's no one to turn to for support.

But don't worry – here's a book that takes you through everything you need to know not only to go freelance, but also to thrive in your career choice.

WHAT'S THIS BOOK ABOUT?

This book aims to guide you through everything you need to know in order to set up and run a successful freelancing business in publishing.

But what do we mean by 'success', by 'freelancing', and by 'publishing' exactly? These terms are all ambiguous. Here's how we've defined them for the purposes of this book:

☐ **Freelancer:** By this we mean someone who's self-employed and works for clients. We aren't talking about contractors (people who move from contract to contract with different companies), but someone who has several clients. Most freelancers will work at least part of the time from home. (For more on the definition of a freelancer, see Chapter 2.)

☐ **Publishing:** When we say publishing we mean the UK book publishing industry. A lot of our advice may well also apply to online publishing, magazine publishing, newspaper publishing, and so on, and to book publishing in other countries, but here our focus is UK book publishing because that's the industry we work in and know well.

☐ **Success:** Success is really a personal thing, and only you can decide what your goals are, but in writing this book our core definition for success has been making a decent living. After all, however great your client or project list, if you're struggling to make ends meet on your income, can you really consider freelancing to be a successful career move?

WHO'S THIS BOOK FOR?

This book is for both wannabe freelancers and existing ones in the publishing industry. It's for anyone who wants to know more about how freelancing works, and how you build a successful career as a freelancer.

You may be:

☐ a freelancer who wants to build their business
☐ a professional who's looking to change career
☐ a retired person looking for a part-time income
☐ a student or recent graduate planning your career
☐ working in-house for a publisher, and considering going freelance.

The beauty of freelancing is that it offers a flexible career choice for a range of people from a range of backgrounds and at differing stages in their careers. This book offers crucial advice and information for anyone who's serious about succeeding as a freelancer.

WHY DID WE WRITE THIS BOOK?

This is the first book on the market that's written for freelancers, by freelancers, that offers a comprehensive guide to setting up and running a thriving freelance business in whichever area of publishing you work – from editorial to design and marketing.

Oh, how we wished a book like this had existed when we went freelance! And we soon discovered we weren't the only freelancers to be frustrated by the lack of information available, especially on freelancing within the publishing industry. So we decided to write a simple, accessible, practical guide to plug this gap in the market and to share the experience we've built over our years of freelancing.

Our main aim in writing this book has been to dispel the 'starving artist' myth that's been pervasive for so many years – that if you're a creative type like a writer, illustrator or designer, you're destined for a life of poverty if you follow your dream and use your gifts. We disagree. The writer subsisting on bread and water while scribbling away in a freezing garret belongs only in the pages of romantic historical fiction. With a little know-how, a good dose of business nous, and a lot of hard graft, there's no reason why you can't make good money as a freelancer.

WHO ARE THE AUTHORS?

Charlie

Books have always been my passion. I was one of those children who was always labouring over poems and stories, who always had her nose in a book, who lived in a world of dragons and big friendly giants, and worlds through wardrobes and pint-sized detectives. All these years later, the stories have changed, but the voracious appetite for literature and writing remains.

I left university as so many students do: utterly clueless about the world of work and what direction I should take. I had the dream of being an author, but knew this wasn't something I intended to pursue as a career; with a sensible head on my shoulders, I knew writing my own books would be something I'd do alongside a job. But what job?

Over the next few years I worked my way through different editorial positions. I started out in PR, then moved to a publishing house, and finally to a charity. In each role I loved the writing, editing, and proofreading work, but there was always something missing for me – challenge, freedom, the choice to focus purely on the work I loved. And I discovered the office environment didn't suit me at all. I felt stifled, bored, and frustrated by the politics and stagnancy and negativity I felt were all around.

Finally, an idea emerged: why not do the work I wanted, but for myself, from home? At first, the idea was ridiculous, terrifying. Was I experienced enough? How on earth did freelancing work? What if I failed terribly and ended up broke and jobless?

Over time, I sat with the idea and it gathered momentum. I read books on self-employment and business. I talked to existing freelancers. I began considering possible business names and marketing strategies and people I could approach for work. Eventually, my doubts receded and I decided I had little to lose. If I tried and failed, I'd simply go out and get another job.

And so, on a cold, dreary January morning, from a corner of the living room of my little flat, I launched Perfectly Write – a business that offered marketing copywriting, copy-editing, and proofreading services. For the following months I worked very hard at building a client base. I set up a website, realized it was rubbish, then set up another, better one. I attended all manner of networking events, and spent countless hours spreading the word of my services online. I went to business training courses, and joined a local creative industries group. And I sent hundreds of letters to publishers, marketing companies, and charities promoting my services.

The first year of business was the hardest, and I took on pretty much anything I was offered in my determination to gain experience, a decent client list, and enough money to make freelancing a viable long-term career choice. But soon my emerging reputation, my growing experience, and my relentless marketing activities paid off. I began building a large, varied client list, working on bigger, more exciting projects, and taking satisfaction in my rising bank balance.

All those years ago, when I first went freelance, I never imagined I would have the successful business I run today. In fact, in going freelance I had made the decision to choose enjoyment in my career over ambition. I had reconciled myself to the idea that I would hopefully earn enough to get by with this job, but realistically, I'd probably make less than I had in my in-house positions. What I hadn't expected was that, for a freelancer, the sky's the limit. If you're determined and focused and business-minded, you can carve an exciting, fulfilling, prosperous career all on your own. For me, nothing beats freelancing – the challenge, the variety, the freedom. I dreamed of a life where I could write and edit for a living, on my terms, in my home, and I made that dream a reality. To quote 'Invictus', 'I am the master of my fate.'

Emma

Like Charlie, I always had my head in a book, and spent my childhood years reading and writing at every given opportunity. Following my English degree, I had the choice of three paths to follow: become an English teacher; do a PhD; or try my hand at writing full-time with a view to winning the Nobel Prize for Literature. Needless to say, I chose none of these paths, and ended up doing a postgraduate course in Business and IT, which led to almost a decade working in the financial world.

They say most of us never follow our true calling in life and I was no exception. Although I knew I wanted to work on books for a living, I simply didn't have the courage to leave the security of my banking role. After all, I was earning lots, lived in a nice place, and could afford decent holidays. Many people would have been perfectly happy to be in my position. But several incidents (and turning 30!) proved to me that I either needed to get out or resign myself to a life of office drudgery. By a strange twist of fate, an author friend of mine asked me to help him out with his manuscript, which I ended up editing and rewriting – and I totally fell in love with the process. Banking versus working on books? No contest.

Knowing that the life of the self-employed didn't guarantee a nice pay cheque at the end of each month, I saved up for a year before I totally threw in the towel. During this time, I signed myself up for every publishing event I could find, subscribed to trade publications, did a few courses, and joined publishing societies. If I was going to make such a dramatic switch in industries, then I needed to know everything there was to know about my next career move. When I felt a bit more confident that I wouldn't starve or be forced to live on the streets by entering into the world of freelancing, I made a very scary choice and walked away from a highly paid executive position in investment banking. It was the best move I ever made.

The first year of any new business is always the hardest, and like Charlie I struggled in the beginning to get enough work in to keep my head above water. My savings came in pretty handy that first year! However, I knew that if I kept at it, my luck would change, and slowly but surely projects started to come my way. I took on mainly editing, proofreading, and copywriting work in the beginning. Although my dream was to become a fully fledged author in my own right, I didn't have the confidence to put myself out there and market myself as a 'brilliant new writer'. However, when I tried my hand at ghostwriting I realized how much I enjoyed it. Meeting new people from all walks of life, researching and learning about different subjects, the travel involved – what's not to like? So, I gradually started to take on more ghosting projects, continuing the editing work but keeping it more as a sideline.

Often, people are fascinated/repelled by ghostwriters, believing they're merely puppets who are hired by celebrities to write books that they're too lazy or stupid to write themselves. However, as I found out, ghostwriting is an extremely tough job, and it's no coincidence that there aren't that many of us out there. It's one of those jobs that you have to absolutely love, as it's as frustrating as it is fascinating.

Through my ghostwriting and copywriting endeavours, I have managed to build enough of a reputation to write books of my own. It feels fantastic to finally be an author, but do I plan on leaving the ghostwriting and editing projects behind? Absolutely not. The joy of freelancing is the variety and freedom it brings, and I would never give that up (well, unless I won the Nobel Prize, of course . . . !).

HOW DO I USE THIS BOOK?

However you like! You can read the book cover to cover, skip to the sections that most apply to you, or dip in and out of it as and when you need guidance.

Here's a rough guide to help you navigate the contents:

- ☐ Chapter 1 helps you to think carefully before going freelance about whether this style of work will suit you.

- ☐ Chapters 2 to 4 deal with the nitty gritty of setting up and running your business, covering legal, financial, administrative and practical concerns.

- ☐ Chapters 5 and 6 help you bring in work through different types of marketing activities.

- ☐ Chapters 7 and 8 are all about the relationships you build – with other freelancers and with clients.

- ☐ Chapter 9 takes you through the various freelancing roles – from proofreading to book critiquing, indexing to graphic design.

- ☐ Chapter 10 closes the book with some case studies of other freelancers whose stories can provide inspiration if you find yourself wondering, *Can I really succeed in freelancing?*

Within each chapter, you'll find some icons that flag up important points:

- ☐ **Alarm Bell:**   Beware! This flags up something you avoid at your peril.

- ☐ **Flashbacks:**   We take a moment to reminisce and share an experience we hope you can learn from.

☐ **Ask Yourself:**   We invite you to ponder for a moment to clarify your thinking.

☐ **Top Tip:**   Denotes a tip you'll find really useful.

And, because we don't pretend to know it all, you'll also find some case studies and information provided by other freelancers and those working in the industry. We hope you're as inspired by these contributors as we've been.

HOW CAN I FIND OUT MORE ABOUT FREELANCING?

Simple: head to our blog at **www.freelancingtips.com**. There we chat about freelancing issues, share more advice, discuss experiences, and pick the brains of other successful freelancers.

1
SUITS YOU, SIR?

When asked what we do for a living, our answer, 'freelancing', is always met with the same response: envy. Many dream of freelancing – of being their own boss, of picking and choosing their projects, of taking time off when they fancy, of working from home. Freelancing conjures up pictures of sleeping late, enjoying boozy lunches in beer gardens, and sprawling on the sofa with the laptop, keeping half an eye on daytime TV. The reality, however, is far removed from this hazy, lazy daydream.

The country is full of freelancers: some happy, successful, and secure; others struggling to make ends meet, to find work, and to manage projects. If you're going to take the big step into freelancing, you want it to be the right decision for you, one that will bring success and fulfilment. You want to go forwards with open eyes and no illusions. Therefore, first you need to know whether you've got what it takes to make it, and then you need to consider carefully the pros and cons of freelancing so that you can make an informed decision. In this chapter we help you do just that. We take you through different aspects of freelancing to help you decide whether this career choice will work for you.

 If you're already freelancing then this chapter can help you clarify whether you're happy on this path, or perhaps need to rethink your direction.

HAVING THE NECESSARY ABILITY

Your starting point is your ability to do the job. There's no point deciding to be a freelance editor if your grammar is appalling. You won't make it as a freelance illustrator if a five-year-old could better your artistic efforts. And you won't be a successful freelance book publicist if the word 'sell' makes you feel wobbly around the knees.

Ability, then, is everything. Some skills can be learned. There are plenty of courses available for those wanting to improve their writing skills, learn how to proofread or index, get to grips with design programmes, or grasp the basics of marketing.

But how successful you'll be at developing your skills depends on your natural ability. You need to have a flair for your specialism. Writers need to have a talent for crafting words. Editors must have a mind that demands structure, sense, and consistency. Graphic designers are artists at heart.

Both of us were born writers. The best way we can describe it is that we have a feel for language. We never needed someone to teach us how to write well. And although we've both done extensive editorial training, often we 'feel' what we need to do with text, rather than considering the technical reasons why.

 Think about the area of service(s) you'd like to offer clients. Do you have a natural flair, a talent, an inherent ability?

We're not asking you to be arrogant, just honest. You may be unsure. That's okay – it's possible to be pretty clueless about your strengths and talents (just think of thousands of talentless wannabes who audition for TV programmes like *The X Factor!*). If in doubt, ask people close to you what they think. Can you write? Can you draw? Can you market something? Can you spot a typo at 40 paces?

Ultimately, it's your ability that will decide your level of success as a freelancer. We're both lucky enough to have a wide range of clients coming back time and time again, and recommending our services, and that needs to be your target as well. Gaining a good reputation and pleasing clients is predominantly down to the quality of the work you produce. The industry is saturated with freelancers, and if you want to be one of those who goes the distance, you need to be darn good at your job.

DRAWING ON EXPERIENCE

People come to freelancing from different backgrounds:

☐ **Career-changers:** You may be doing just about anything – PA, artist, estate agent, and so on. You're starting afresh.

☐ **Out of work:** You may be unemployed, a recent graduate, retired, or a stay-at-home parent. You may have a background in publishing and/or in a particular specialism, or you may be a complete newbie.

☐ **Publishing in-housers:** You may work for a publisher, perhaps as an editor or cover designer, or you may work for a printer as a typesetter. You're looking to make the move to working for yourself.

☐ **Side-steppers:** You may already carry out an editorial or design role at work, but in a different sector to book publishing. For example, you may work as a writer in a PR agency, or a graphic designer for a corporate communications department. You want to continue your role, but in the publishing world.

Whatever your career history, the likelihood for any new freelancer is that you lack varied and extensive experience in your chosen field of book publishing. At best, you've been an in-house editor for several different publishers; at worst, you're changing careers from accountant to writer and you've never been paid to write a word in your life.

The problem is, clients like freelancers who have a proven track record of working for publishers and delivering good-quality work on time and on budget. The newbie freelancer faces a chicken-and-egg dilemma: you need experience to get jobs, but only jobs bring experience.

First, be reassured that you can make it as a freelancer without many years of experience in the industry behind you. Charlie worked in PR and as an editor at one publisher before going freelance; Emma worked in marketing in the investment banking sector. If you already have some experience in publishing and/or your chosen role, then you have a good starting point.

But the hard truth is, if you have very little or no experience, you're going to find establishing yourself as a freelancer a challenge. There are ways to improve your CV – put together a portfolio that showcases your talents, do some voluntary work (charities are always pleased for you to donate your skills), take on some corporate-sector projects. But you may have to work extra hard to get clients to give you a break.

 If you're lacking experience, are you prepared to make sacrifices to gain some? Can you start at the bottom and accept that, at first, you may be doing projects that don't excite you? If it comes to it, are you prepared to put off freelancing for now so that you can gain some more experience in-house?

Alarm Bell

Newbie freelancers can seldom command the same fee as experienced ones. When you first start out, you may do some low paid or (dare we say it) unpaid work. But you really mustn't accept rubbish pay for long. Working for peanuts doesn't do yourself, or freelancers in general, any good. Take a look at Chapter 4 for more on setting reasonable rates.

THINKING ABOUT QUALIFICATIONS

Many people who contact us for advice on freelancing ask what qualifications they need. The honest answer? Probably none at all.

Clients are much more interested in your natural ability and experience than your educational background or training history. In the entire course of our freelancing careers, no client has ever asked us what A levels we got, or what our degrees were in (in case you're interested, English and Spanish for Emma, American Studies for Charlie). And although we've both done editorial training courses, no client has ever asked us about them.

If you feel you need to develop your skills, by all means do a course. But don't feel that it's essential to success.

LOVING YOUR JOB

Do you have a real passion for books, for publishing, for writing or editing or marketing or designing?

Successful freelancers put their hearts into what they do. Most freelancers in publishing are passionate about books – their words or design. We believe we have the best jobs in the world, because every day we get to make money by simply doing what we enjoy. And nothing beats picking up a title in a bookshop and knowing you helped to create that book.

Your love for proofreading, editing, designing, or whatever you do, comes across in your work. Clients can tell that you take your job seriously, that you care about the standards of your work. And it's nice to work with people who are enthusiastic about their jobs.

Passion is also essential for business success because it's what sustains you during the hard times. Only because you love your job can you pick yourself up after disappointment and carry on. What's the point in running your own business if you don't enjoy it?

A love of illustration or writing or editing or any other publishing service is essential for freelancing, but it will only take you so far. Before taking the plunge and going freelance, make sure you have the practical skills to complement your passion for the work. Otherwise you may well end up like the proverbial starving writer in a draughty, bleak garret.

DONNING YOUR BUSINESS CAP

Gone are the days when the word 'freelancer' denoted a white-haired editor slowly marking up proofs in her chintzy armchair, earning a pittance for her efforts (not familiar with that image? Well, we certainly met our share of these old-schoolers.). Today's freelancer is a new breed: technologically savvy, ambitious, and business-minded.

The key to success is to treat your freelancing as a business.

The way you run your freelancing is just the same as how you'd run any other small business, from book shop to doggy grooming parlour. That means you:

- ☐ are accountable for the work you produce
- ☐ are the boss and, as such, act like one
- ☐ build positive client relationships
- ☐ charge competitive rates
- ☐ clearly define your service
- ☐ deliver work on time, and to the expected standard
- ☐ ensure you're available for contact with clients
- ☐ make 'professional' your middle name
- ☐ operate an organized accounts system
- ☐ pay tax to Her Majesty's Revenue & Customs.

So, if your fantasy of life as a freelancer is sleeping late every day, turning the phone off for a week, doing work when you fancy (rather than when it's due), and pocketing plenty of cash without worrying about such tedious details as invoices and tax returns, you're in for a nasty shock. A successful freelancer needs to have all the attributes of a successful businessperson: tenacious; sensible; flexible; resilient; organized; driven; ambitious; and one hell of a grafter.

BEING YOUR OWN BOSS

When you freelance, you are the business, therefore you have to fulfil all the roles you'd expect to find at work, such as:

- ☐ accounts person
- ☐ administrator
- ☐ boss
- ☐ office cleaner.

That means if a client's not happy, you can't run to your boss for help. If an invoice is overdue, there's no accounts person to chase payment. And if the carpet's thick with dust, no vacuum-wielding lady in a pinny is going to take care of it for you (unless your granny's visiting, perhaps).

Of course, freelancing doesn't mean you're completely without support. You can befriend other freelancers and ask their advice, and you can get support for financial and business development matters from organizations such as Business Link.

But ultimately, you're in charge, and for some people that can be a scary proposition. The success or failure of the business is entirely down to you. No more moaning about the boss or the organization you work for; no more frittering away time gossiping at the water cooler or covertly surfing the net; no more giving it just 70 per cent. Freelancing strips everything away and lays you, your skills, your abilities, and your ambitions bare.

Successful freelancers often thrive on the challenge of working for themselves, and say they could never go back to being employed. There's a strong feeling of pride – every success you have and every penny you earn is down to your own hard work.

DEALING WITH FINANCIAL UNCERTAINTY

The fear that holds most people back from going freelance is money, or to be more precise, the potential lack of it. We all have a particular lifestyle we either enjoy or aspire to, and we want our jobs to safely fund the house, the car, the clothes, the food, the holiday, the cappuccino habit.

Of course, it is possible to make decent money as a freelancer (we wouldn't be writing this book if that were not the case), but no matter how successful your freelancing business, you'll always live with a degree of financial uncertainty.

When you first go freelance, it will no doubt be a budget-frozen-pizza time. Work will come in sporadically, and you'll find yourself lying in bed at night frantically doing calculations and questioning your choice of career. As your business grows, the anxiety will dissipate a little, and you'll upgrade to a nice fresh pizza from the supermarket. But you'll still have dry spells and black moments when you check your bank balance. Finally, when you're up and running as a freelancer, the worry will be less still. But even then, as you tuck into your pizza takeaway blowout, a little voice in your head whispers, 'Where's the next project coming from, the next cheque? And what were you thinking ordering pepperoni *and* tuna topping?'

 Can you live with the constant worry and insecurity of freelancing? It's no good going freelance if the financial uncertainty will tie you up in knots and make you miserable.

When you're employed, life is simple. You know exactly how much you'll be paid once a month, and you budget accordingly. Being self-employed as a freelancer is very different:

- ☐ **Invoice timing:** Projects have different timescales, and you often find yourself invoicing several at once, then invoicing nothing for a couple of months. So, one month your income may be thousands, and the next a big fat zero.

- ☐ **Leaves of absence:** Holidays are unpaid, and you have no protection if you're unable to work – no full-pay sick leave or benefits. For example, when Charlie's son was taken seriously ill, she had no choice but to stop work. The government deemed her ineligible for any assistance, so for three months her income was non-existent. Her husband, meanwhile, who's employed, received four weeks' compassionate leave on full pay. A big difference.

☐ **Tax:** The taxman has dibs on around a third of your income. Woe betide the freelancer who doesn't set aside that share for tax, and instead blows it on some nice new sofas. Further down the road that's going to be a costly, if comfy, mistake.

There are two ways to cope with this financial insecurity:

☐ **The ostrich approach:** Bury your head in the sand. Try not to think too much about money – how you spend it and where it's coming from. Shove your bank statements down the back of your (plush new) sofa and hope for the best.

☐ **The strict-but-sensible approach:** Get a firm grip on your finances, make a budget, and watch those pennies. Only when you're sure you have a decent surplus in the bank do you go out and splurge (guilt-free, because you know you're free to spend).

If you're someone who handles money wisely, you have a good chance of succeeding as a freelancer. But if, on the other hand, money has a nasty habit of slipping through your fingers like a bar of soap in the bath, you're unlikely to manage the financial balancing that freelancing requires in the long term.

Alarm Bell

Consider the financial aspect very seriously before you make a decision to go freelance. If you can't manage your money, you could end up in serious debt.

HANDLING TECHNOLOGY

Ten years ago, many publishers liked to work on paper and by snail mail, and many freelancers could get away with just a touch of word processing here and there. Nowadays, it's a very different story.

At a minimum, all freelancers need to be proficient in:

- ☐ email
- ☐ Microsoft Office applications, e.g. Word and Excel
- ☐ navigating the internet (and researching effectively online).

You may also need to use the following types of software:

- ☐ anti-virus
- ☐ back-up
- ☐ design
- ☐ file sharing
- ☐ indexers
- ☐ PDF editing/creation (Adobe)
- ☐ website design and update.

> If you're determined to go freelance, but you suspect your IT skills aren't up to speed, don't let that hold you back. Attend evening classes, or take an online course. And remember that you can claim the cost of your training as a business expense (see Chapter 4).

COPING WITH EBB AND FLOW

Sometimes, you'll be drowning in work; sometimes, you'll be twiddling your thumbs. Rarely do freelancers have just the right workload.

Take a look at this conversation:

Emma:	Help! I've got so much on I don't know how I'm going to get through it. I was up until midnight last night, and when I went to bed I couldn't sleep because I was so stressed.
Charlie:	That's not good. You'd better not take on anything else for now.
Emma:	Tell me about it, but that XYZ publisher offered me another job, and I said yes. Silly, I know, as I'm already pushed to the max, but for all I know next month will be dead.
Charlie:	True. I'm having a quiet spell. There are projects in the pipeline, but I don't have anything to do today. It's quite nice, though, as I've been so busy lately. Sixty-hour weeks take it out of you. But I hope something comes along soon, all the same.

This is the kind of typical chat we've had day in, day out, for years. The extremes of over-working and not working at all are pretty common, and we've learnt to ride them well.

So, being a freelancer means being prepared to work incredibly hard sometimes, and to put in long hours (we're not joking about the 60-hour week). It also means accepting the quiet times without plunging into a panic. You can use the lulls effectively to bring in more work, catch up on admin, or take some time out before work piles up again.

Ultimately, then, a freelancer needs to be flexible. A successful freelancer isn't deterred by this ebb and flow of work. Rather, they relish the challenge of a busy week, and revel in the tranquility of a quiet one.

ORGANIZING YOUR WORKLOAD

Most freelancers have multiple projects running at any one time. This is the best way to ensure a regular flow of money, after all. And most freelancing projects are relatively small, taking anything from a couple of hours to a couple of weeks, so it's possible to handle many at the same time.

For example, as we write this, Charlie has four other jobs on her to-do list: ghostwriting a children's book chapter; proofreading a book on politics; consistency-checking some chick-lit novels; and editing a title on anxiety. On top of these projects, there are ten more on the 'coming soon' list.

So, if you want to be a freelancer, you'll need to be an ace juggler. Not only are you juggling different projects and their different deadlines, but you need to keep in contact with several different clients at one time. And each client needs to feel that their work is a priority for you (even if the truth is you haven't even looked at his or her book yet).

 How good a juggler are you? Can you multi-task? Can you handle the mental strain of having several different jobs on at the same time? Can you keep momentum on a big project and break it down into manageable chunks?

To manage your workload, you need to be able to gauge how long tasks will take you and then prioritize them effectively. And you need to have the ability to chop and change between projects. You don't always have the luxury of immersing yourself in one project until it's done. Sometimes in a working day you may do a little on two or three different projects.

HANDLING REJECTION

Freelancers need to have a thick skin, determination, and a positive approach. Just as with any other business, rejection or failure (if this is how you choose to define these experiences) abound.

The following sections explore some situations in which you may face rejection.

Approaching a potential client

When Charlie first went freelance, she wrote over 200 letters to publishers in the UK, introducing herself and asking to be added to their freelance list. The response? Five new clients or – depending on your attitude – 195 rejections.

Freelancers have to be glass-half-full people. Five new clients is excellent news! And freelancers have to be tenacious. In fact, in direct marketing terms 5 in 200 is a very good response rate. Building a solid client base takes time, and a hell of a lot of work.

Pitching for a project

Many clients will ask several freelancers for a quote on a project. No matter how superb your pitch, and how exemplary your background and skills, you won't always win the project. The key is not to take this personally.

For example, a government agency once asked Charlie to carry out a sample edit and provide a quote for editing copy, which she did. Eventually the agency came back and told Charlie they weren't offering her the work because her quote came in too high for their budget. However, they admitted that Charlie's sample edit was of a far higher standard than the other, cheaper, editor they were hiring. And, in view of this, the agency would be reviewing their budgets for the future. Charlie wasn't remotely bothered that she hadn't been offered the work. In fact, she was pleased that she'd held to her quote because, after all, quality comes at a price.

As a freelancer you'll quote for many projects. How will you feel when you're not chosen for a project? Frustrated? Hard-done-by? Injured? Or could you take it on the chin as being part and parcel of the business world?

Dealing with client feedback

There will always be times when a client isn't happy with the work you've delivered – the chapter you wrote, the index you created, the book cover you designed – and will tell you so (hopefully, in a professional manner, but sadly not always).

This is where a freelancer needs the hide of a rhino. All freelancers in publishing are engaged in creative work, working with either words or images. And it's easy to be precious about creative endeavours, and feel stung by criticism. It can be pretty heartbreaking to rewrite a page you know is beautifully worded, or to scrap a design you know is perfect. But the client is paying you to do what they want, not what you want, and like it or not you have to defer to their wishes. You have to abide by the golden rule of business: the customer is always right...

...except when the customer is wrong! If the client is moving the goal-posts, you need to stamp this out, or have factored in an element of faffing when you costed the project.

It's essential to put in place procedures to protect yourself from clients who'll argue with you over the work you deliver. You need to clearly define your services, and create terms and conditions and a project agreement for the client to sign. Chapter 5 helps you do this.

BEING A PEOPLE-PERSON

Freelancers get on with people. They may work from home, alone, but that doesn't mean they're timid mice or recluses.

You've got to be a friendly sort to build a client base. No one wants to work with a stiff, boring, standoffish freelancer. Clients would much prefer to send a project to someone with a bit of life and humour.

That said, successful freelancers also understand the importance of not overstepping the mark and being too familiar. Freelancers are professional. Think service with a smile.

 Do you like working with people from all walks of life and different backgrounds? Can you be respectful, polite and non-judgemental of clients? How would you react if a client was rude – could you remain professional?

WORKING FROM HOME

The vast majority of freelancers work from home, either all or part of the time. After all, that's one of the major attractions of this style of work. No doubt your mind is already awash with the advantages of being at home as you work. You can:

- ☐ catch *Neighbours* at lunchtime
- ☐ check out Facebook whenever you want
- ☐ control your environment (heat, light, space, noise and so on)
- ☐ get from 'home' to 'work' in ten seconds flat
- ☐ have a beer
- ☐ keep the dog company
- ☐ let in tradesmen (and keep a beady eye on them)
- ☐ lie in
- ☐ listen to music as you work
- ☐ phone friends whenever you like
- ☐ sit in the garden while you eat lunch
- ☐ take deliveries
- ☐ work in your pyjamas.

Sounds good, eh? Sadly, it's not all roses. Working from home can be:

☐ **Boring:** The same old desk, the same old view, the same old four walls. Yawn.

☐ **Distracting:** It's amazing how little things can chip away at your work time – ringing the bank, hanging the washing out, ordering an online food shop, unpacking the online food shop, eating the contents of the online food shop, eavesdropping on your neighbour having a blazing row with her husband in the back garden . . . Sometimes, home isn't the oasis of calm and hub of productivity you'd like it to be.

☐ **Isolating:** Your Christmas party is you, a mince pie, a cracker, and a party hat. Very nice, but not a patch on people and chat and laughter.

☐ **Lonely:** Me, myself, and I can be pretty tedious company, and by the time your partner comes home you may find your voice is strangely squeaky from disuse.

Working from home isn't for everyone. If you want to freelance but you suspect you aren't cut out to be home alone all day, consider hiring office space. It's an added expense, but it means you get out each day and can clearly separate your work and home life.

Nowadays, some creative freelancers and small businesses – such as animators, designers, artists and writers – like to share work space to have company but also inspiration and ready sounding boards for ideas.

BALANCING HOME AND WORK

Before going freelance, it's wise to consider how this style of work would fit with your home life.

 How would freelancing affect your partner and/or kids? Would you have more time to spend with them, or less? Would you be able to effectively separate work and play? Would your household cope with the uncertainty of your income?

Many people go freelance because it allows more time to be with children. For example, Charlie works from 9a.m. to 3p.m., Monday to Friday, while her son is in nursery, and then does some hours in the evenings and at weekends while her husband is home to help out. Working a short day reduces the cost of childcare, and means her son has more 'mummy time'.

However, Charlie's set-up isn't always easy. Rather than go to work five days a week, Charlie works some hours every day of the week. Rather than do all her work in one flow, Charlie might do an hour early morning, a few hours in the day, then several in the evening. And rather than coming home from the office free of work, Charlie has to try to switch off at home while knowing that work awaits behind the office door.

For freelancers there's always work to be done – whether it's client work, marketing to find more work, or mundane admin. Giving yourself permission to stop and have 'home-time' is hard. But you have to rein in the temptation to become a workaholic and keep balance in your life.

CONSIDERING YOUR HEALTH

Freelancing can be either a help or a hindrance to keeping healthy, depending on your experience.

Some freelancers take advantage of the flexibility of the job to build more exercise into their daily routine, such as a trip to the gym or a swim. After all, the lack of a commute to work creates more time in the day. And some ditch the junk food because they now have time to create delicious, nutritious meals from scratch. These are very motivated, wise people.

Unfortunately, in our experience, when it comes to healthy living, people aren't often motivated or wise. And freelancing can make it that bit harder to stay healthy:

☐ **Eating:** The biscuit jar calls to you. It's just a few steps from your desk, and there are no colleagues to watch, appalled, as you devour five digestives in a minute flat.

☐ **Exercise:** Working from home means you drastically reduce the amount you move about. It's not uncommon to stop work and realize the farthest you've been all day is to the bathroom or the kitchen.

As with other aspects of freelancing, you need to find self-control and motivation. Freelancing can open a door to a healthier you, but if you're someone who has a tendency to slip into couch potato habits, you need to consider how working at home will affect you.

SUMMARY

Freelancing may suit you if you're:

✓ a people-person

✓ able to separate work and play

✓ assertive

✓ business-minded

✓ flexible

✓ good at managing money

✓ happy in your own company

✓ hard-working

✓ highly organized

✓ independent

✓ motivated

✓ passionate about books and your specialisms

✓ resilient

✓ self-motivated

✓ tenacious.

2

SETTING UP SHOP

So, you've decided to go freelance. Congratulations! Now you can begin paving the way for your new business.

In this chapter we help you find your feet as a self-employed person and prepare you for trading. When you actually come to it, becoming a freelancer is surprisingly simple: you just tell the government you're now self-employed. Of course, you've a long way to go before you're bringing in clients and making money, but after you cover the elements of this chapter, you're officially self-employed, you've set up a comfortable workspace for your business, and you're ready to move on to the all-important work of marketing your business (see Chapters 5 and 6). You've laid the foundations for prosperous, rewarding freelancing.

CONSIDERING YOUR TIMING

Picture the scenario: you've had an exciting weekend weighing up the pros and cons of freelancing, and deciding it's definitely right for you. You're on a high – exhilarated, inspired, full of ideas and motivation. You sail into work Monday morning, march into your boss's office, and say, 'Good morning. I quit. I'm going freelance. See ya!' Cut to two weeks later and you're at home worriedly twiddling a pencil as you stare at the blank screen of your PC. No clients. No work. No money. No hope of paying the mortgage. Oops.

Going freelance is just like setting up any business – it takes time and a lot of planning. If you want to keep hold of your sanity and avoid sinking into debt, you need to find the most secure path for transitioning from whatever work you're doing now (assuming you are working) to becoming a full-time freelancer.

Setting up while still employed

You can carry out some setting-up tasks in your free time while still working in your current job:

- ☐ deciding on your business name
- ☐ designing a website
- ☐ designing and printing stationery, such as business cards
- ☐ finding an accountant
- ☐ opening a business bank account
- ☐ organizing your workspace
- ☐ preparing marketing activities such as a mailshot.

You can even start advertising your services, and take on some client projects while still working full-time for an employer (remember to tell HMRC as soon as you start self-employed work; see the later section 'Registering as self-employed').

Alarm Bell

If you currently work in the publishing industry, moonlighting as a freelancer can be problematic. Your boss may not be impressed to discover, while sourcing a freelancer, that you're advertising without their knowledge. And approaching the clients you work with in your day job could land you in hot water. For example, if you work in a publishing recruitment agency and are going freelance as an editor, you may be in breach of your employment contract to approach one of the agency's clients on the sly and ask for work. Those who work in publishing should consider being open about their move to freelancing.

Making the move to full-time

How long you balance your existing job and your emerging business depends on how your business evolves.

Charlie, for example, quit her job pretty quickly after getting some initial work from clients because she found her employment was sapping time and energy she wanted to devote to the business. For a couple of months she did both part-time temp work and her client work, until eventually clients were consistently sending work, and she was earning more month on month. Knowing her husband's salary would cover their main outgoings if the business struggled, Charlie finally quit the temp job and went full-time.

The bottom line is this: before you can go full-time on your business, you need to make sure it's financially viable. Going freelance is never going to be easy at first – it's likely that you'll struggle financially for a while, and will have to clamp down on spending. But you must make sure that although money will be tight, it won't be non-existent.

If you think you're ready to go full-time, ask yourself:

- ☐ Will I afford my rent or mortgage?
- ☐ Will I pay my bills – utilities, mobile, loan repayments?
- ☐ Will I afford basic essentials – train fares, toilet roll, shampoo?
- ☐ Will I be able to afford eating healthily?
- ☐ Will I have enough leeway for the unexpected – a broken boiler, an absence from work due to illness?

Ideally, you have some savings or you have a partner who's able to cover your basic outgoings. If you don't have financial backing like this, you'll have to be very sure that you have a solid enough client base to guarantee sufficient earnings.

The beauty of freelancing is that you can pick and choose your hours. If you've quit your job and gone full-time with your business, but you're not doing as well as you'd hoped, do something about your dwindling income. Get a part-time job, or some temp work to tide you over. All that matters is keeping your head above water while you work to develop the business.

CHECKING THAT YOU WILL BE SELF-EMPLOYED

Once you're ready to go freelance, you're entering the world of self-employment. First of all, you need to understand exactly what that means.

In this book we use the term 'freelancer' to mean someone who's self-employed and who works for several different clients. The freelancer may work from home or at rented premises, or may sometimes work in-house for a client.

However, some people who call themselves freelancers are actually employed, not self-employed. Usually these are people who take on lengthy contracts with one company, work solely for that company during the contract, and then move on to a contract at another company.

If you aren't sure whether you'll be self-employed, take a look at the following questions. A self-employed freelancer answers 'Yes' to every one of these questions:

☐ Do you have several clients?

☐ Do you set your rates?

☐ Do you decide if, when, and where to work?

☐ Do you have business premises? *(Note: this can mean your home)*

☐ Do you buy and maintain your own work equipment?

☐ Do you work without bonuses, overtime, holiday, or sick pay?

Alarm Bell

HMRC is very particular about you getting your employment status right. If you're registered as employed when you're actually self-employed, you aren't paying tax correctly. And if you try to pass yourself off as self-employed when you aren't, you're taking advantage of the benefits this status brings, such as the ability to claim expenses against your tax liability. Either way, get this wrong and you'll be in hot water with the tax authorities.

Sometimes it's not as cut and dried as being either self-employed or employed: you can be both at the same time. For example, if you do some temp work to tide you over during the early, cash-strapped days of your business, you're receiving both employed and self-employed earnings.

 If you're in any doubt, call HMRC and ask for advice. They can untangle the most complicated of circumstances with you.

DETERMINING YOUR BUSINESS STRUCTURE

There are different legal structures you can adopt when setting up a business. The ones freelancers need to understand are sole trading and limited companies.

Being a sole trader

Self-employed freelancers operate as sole traders. This is the legal business structure that basically means you are your business – the business legally has no separate existence from you, its owner.

The sole trader structure is very simple:

☐ **Accounts:** Very straightforward. You pretty much just log what's coming in and what's going out.

☐ **Costs:** It costs nothing to register as self-employed, and you don't need to get an accountant if you don't want to.

☐ **Earnings:** All the money the business makes, minus tax, goes straight into your pocket.

☐ **Liability:** If your business owes money, you're personally accountable for the debt. So, if you run up a huge debt, then the debt collectors may come knocking at your front door. However, this downside is unlikely to apply to a freelancer in publishing, whose business outgoings (and thus the possibility of debt) are minor.

☐ **Set up:** Easy peasy. All you need to do is ring HMRC and have a short conversation in which you announce you're self-employed (see the later section 'Registering as self-employed').

☐ **Tax:** You fill in an annual tax return and pay tax twice a year through the self-assessment scheme. You also pay Class 2 National Insurance weekly.

☐ **Terminating:** Closing the business is as easy as starting it. You tell HMRC you've ceased trading, and pay any remaining tax when it's due.

Setting up a limited company

Although the vast majority of freelancers in publishing are sole traders, a few choose to trade within a limited company that they set up.

The limited liability company structure has two benefits:

☐ When your income rises above a certain level, then trading through a limited company rather than as a sole trader can save you money on your tax bill. You'd need an accountant to determine at what point it would be cheaper to become a limited company, but broadly speaking it's often if you fall into the higher tax bracket.

☐ Owning a limited liability company means you have limited liability for business debts. If your business is in trouble, this may (but won't necessarily) save you from bankruptcy.

So, freelancers consistently earning at a high level, or those who are worried about liability, may decide to trade with a limited company. But these usually are freelancers who've been trading for years as sole traders.

Alarm Bell

You should never set up a limited company without doing your homework and getting expert financial advice. Limited companies involve a lot of paperwork, cost more to run (accountant and registration fees), and are complicated to set up, run, and close.

Don't worry about limited companies if you're only just starting out; stick to the sole trader route. It's useful to be aware of different business structures for the future, but being a sole trader is the simple, easy option.

REGISTERING AS SELF-EMPLOYED

Within three months of starting their business, sole traders must register it with HMRC. Failure to do so leads to a £100 fine. Sometimes the exact start date for a business can be debatable, so register as soon as possible to avoid paying a penalty.

Here's how to register as self-employed:

- □ **Online:** Go to www.hmrc.gov.uk/selfemployed.
- □ **Phone:** Call the Newly Self-Employed Helpline on 0845 915 4515.
- □ **Post:** Fill in and post form CWFA (www.hmrc.gov.uk/forms/cwf1.pdf).

You'll need to provide the following information:

- □ address (personal and business, if different)
- □ date of birth
- □ email address (personal and business, if different)
- □ name
- □ National Insurance number
- □ phone number (personal and business, if different)
- □ the date your self-employment commenced
- □ the nature of your business.

 Keep a record of the date you register as self-employed, as you will need this in later tax returns.

SETTING UP CLASS 2 NATIONAL INSURANCE PAYMENTS

The bad news is, once you register as self-employed you have to start paying tax straightaway. The good news is, the Class 2 National Insurance charge is only around £2.40 per week.

When you register as self-employed, HMRC will send you a form, or ask you to fill in details online, to set up your payment for this tax. You usually pay it monthly by Direct Debit.

CHOOSING A BUSINESS NAME

If you want, you can simply trade in your own name. Some freelancers like the simplicity and personal nature of this approach, and it particularly suits writers and illustrators who want to be known for their work. For example, Emma simply trades as Emma Murray.

Alternatively, you may decide you'd like to trade under a business name, which gives a corporate feel and helps convey to a potential client the nature of your business. You can then use the business name for branding and marketing activities. As long as you include your own name (which the business is registered to) on marketing materials and important documents such as invoices and project agreements, HMRC are happy for you to operate with a business name. Officially, you are 'Your Name trading as Your Business's Name'.

When choosing a business name, bear in mind that you're going to have to live (and work) with this name for a long time. For example, Charlie rues the day she called her business 'Perfectly Write'. Although it seemed fun at the time and summed up a commitment to high standards, the fact is that no one is perfect – every proofreader misses the odd error; every writer makes the odd typo. Nowadays, Charlie would much prefer to work under a name that suggests she's good at her job, but not impossibly faultless. But changing the name of an established business isn't easy, and you run the risk of damaging marketing activities and confusing clients.

Here are some things to consider when coming up with your business name:

☐ **Be realistic and grounded.** Don't get carried away and call yourself something like 'The National Association of Words' – apart from being too grand, you aren't allowed to use words like 'association' and 'national' in a business name without government permission!

☐ **Check no one else is using the name.** You can use the same business name as another business as long as it's not a trademark (for example, Charlie recently discovered a freelancer trading under Perfectly Write in the US). But where possible it's best to be original. The Business Link website (www.businesslink.gov.uk) has a useful tool for checking whether company names are in use and/or trademarked – just type 'company name and trade mark checker' into the search box.

☐ **Embody your business.** Choose a name that conveys the nature of your business. For example, the name 'The Book Writer' clearly conveys that the business deals with book writing. Conversely, a business name like 'Blue Monkey' does nothing to explain who you are and what you do. And a name like 'RG Marketing' does convey that you deal with marketing, but not specifically book marketing, so you may be confused with a marketing agency.

☐ **Keep it concise.** A name like 'Amanda Brown's Professional Proofreading, Editing, and Writing Services' is a bit of a mouthful.

☐ **Make it memorable.** 'Perfectly Write' may not be the perfect name, but over the years Charlie's had plenty of comments on it.

☐ **Make sure it's easy to spell.** Not all clients would find it easy to type an email to bob@specializededitorialising.com.

PREPARING YOUR WORK ENVIRONMENT

Imagine you're setting up a new company. You look at several offices before picking one that you think will suit your needs. Then you work to make that office as comfortable and fit-for-purpose as possible for yourself and your new employees. You may section off some space, add some better lighting, and get the dodgy radiators fixed. You'll buy (or lease) the best phones, IT equipment, and furniture. You'll check there are no trailing leads to trip on, that screen glare is minimized, that chairs allow people to sit in the correct posture at their desks, because you're responsible for health and safety.

Setting up as a freelancer is just the same as starting any new business, except for most freelancers your business premises double as your home. You can run a business from the kitchen table, vying for space amid crockery and the kids' homework, shoving paperwork here, there, and everywhere. But you're unlikely to reach your full potential by writing or editing or designing at a 'desk' in such chaotic, distracting surroundings.

Putting some effort into creating a dedicated workspace that's clean, comfortable, and uncluttered helps get you in the mindset of a successful, serious professional, and gives you space to be organized, focused, efficient, and creative – all essential for successful freelancing.

Designating workspace

Assuming that you work from home and aren't renting office space, you need to find a part of your home you can dedicate to your business.

Creating a discrete office

The easiest option is to set aside an entire room for work – a spare bedroom, a study, your converted garage, the garden shed. Size isn't important; all you're looking for is four walls and a door to close.

Using a separate room for work has two benefits:

☐ **Focus:** You designate this space for work, and while in the room you have no distractions.

☐ **Switching off:** The line between work and home is less blurred, because your workspace is segregated from the home, and you can close the door on work at the end of the day, both physically and metaphorically.

Alarm Bell

HMRC has strict rules about claiming expenses for working from home. If you devote an entire room solely to business, you may be liable to pay Capital Gains Tax. To avoid this tax, always keep the room you designate for your business as having a second function – for example, Charlie's office contains a sofa-bed – and only claim expenses for using part of the room. Flip to Chapter 4 for more on tax and expenses.

Squishing into a family room

Of course, some people don't have the luxury of commandeering an entire room for business. Lack of space forces some people to set up a desk in the living room, dining room, kitchen, or a bedroom.

This arrangement may suit you fine. Perhaps it's warmer or lighter in the living room, or you want to set up on the kitchen table so you can keep an eye on the kids when they're home and you are within easy reach of the kettle.

Some freelancers, however, find it a challenge to work productively and comfortably in a workspace that's blended into their home. There are so many more distractions, especially if you're trying to work when other people are in the house – 'Mum, where's the biscuits?', 'Dad, Dad, come and see!', 'Darling, did you post those letters?' And because you're sharing your space, there's always the risk that a family member will accidentally (or otherwise) trash your work – spill tea on your keyboard, delete an important file, put sticky jam paw-prints on your proofs.

Then there's the problem of time off. Freelancers tend to find it difficult to switch off at the best of times, but when your work is staring you in the face while you cook dinner, watch *EastEnders*, or try to sleep, it's very difficult to enjoy guilt-free you-time.

 If you can't have a separate room for your business, try to section off the office space you do have. A strategically placed bookshelf or screen can make a big difference.

Choosing furniture

Happily, your furniture needs are very simple:

- ☐ **Chair:** Make it a comfy one because you're going to be sitting on it a lot. Swivel chairs with wheels can make life easier for moving about (or, on a quiet afternoon, spinning until you're giddy). Your chair either needs to be the right height for the desk, or be adjustable, and an adjustable backrest (height and slant) is also desirable. If you can't reach to rest your feet flat on the floor, get a footrest.

- ☐ **Desk:** The bigger, the better, we say. You need room for your computer peripherals (monitor, keyboard, mouse, printer), a lamp, and to spread out papers.

- ☐ **Storage:** Bookcases, filing cabinets, shelves, boxes – the choice is yours. Just give yourself a place for organizing books, papers, files, and other odds and ends for the business.

Once you've set up your desk and chair, you can put on your occupational health hat and carry out a workstation assessment. Adjust your chair height and the placement of your monitor so that your forearms are roughly horizontal and your eyes are level with the top of the screen.

Getting techy

No freelancer can get away with a purely paper-based office. You're going to need some basic technology to do your job, and perhaps some extra gadgets to make life a little easier.

The bare essentials

Here's a list of must-haves:

- ☐ **Computer:** How high-spec your computer is depends on your needs. You want a reliable machine that has sufficient memory and a fast enough processor to keep up with your pace. And you need to put in place a foolproof back-up procedure (see Chapter 3).

- ☐ **Phone:** Even if you prefer to email correspondence, there will always be occasions when a client wants to chat. You can use your home landline, have a separate line put in, use your personal mobile, or buy a work one.

- ☐ **Printer:** The quality very much depends on the nature of your work. Proofreaders, for example, will often need to print long documents, and graphic designers may want to print high resolution images. If you're buying a new printer, take care to consider the cost of cartridges – the printer may be cheap as chips, but is the ink?

Optional gizmos and gadgets

These techy bits can be handy, but they aren't essential for running your business:

□ **Answerphone:** If you don't have a voicemail function on your phone, you'll need a way to capture clients' messages.

□ **Speakerphone:** This can be a useful addition to your home phone when interviewing clients or conducting conference calls.

□ **Dictaphone:** Recording your interviews is much more reliable than using a notepad and pen.

□ **External hard drive:** An excellent way to store files, helping you free up space on your computer and providing a reliable back-up.

□ **Fax:** We've never needed to use one; a scanner and email work as a substitute. But you may like to add this to your office paraphernalia.

□ **Photocopier:** Pretty handy, but you might not use it much so don't go buying an enormous office one. Most printers these days come with the function.

□ **Scanner:** Like the photocopier, this is a useful tool that printers often incorporate. We find it handy for cutting down postage – printing off purchase orders, signing them, and then emailing back to the client.

□ **Second computer:** A life-saver if your main computer loses the will to live. The second computer doesn't need to be fancy: an old, reliable one will do.

□ **Shredder:** Chucking your business bank statements and confidential client documents in the rubbish is risky in this day and age. A decent shredder helps you dispose of your waste safely (and makes excellent bedding for the hamster's cage).

□ **Smartphone:** You may decide you'd like to be mobile with your business, picking up emails in the supermarket and posting items to your blog or social networking pages.

Weighing up laptop versus PC

Whether you work on a laptop or PC is entirely a matter of personal choice. Here's how the two compare:

Laptop	PC
More portable	Cheaper
More compact	Bigger screen
	Bigger keyboard

Alarm Bell

A laptop gives you the freedom to work in many different places (battery willing). But don't get carried away working here, there, and everywhere. It may be good fun laying out a book in a coffee shop, or writing on the train now and then, but you'll find you aren't as efficient or accurate working in places with distractions. And working on a laptop all day long can also cause back pain and bad posture!

Organizing your workspace

Part of the job of freelancing is having the freedom to work as you like. There's no boss complaining about the state of your desk, tutting at your chaotic filing system, or giving you a ticking off because you've lost an important document somewhere in the chaos that is your workspace.

But efficiency is everything in the business world, because time is money. The more time you spend on administrative tasks, the less time you have for your client work. We know of freelancers who've had to turn down work (and thus money) at tax return time because their paperwork was such a mess that they needed to set aside days to sort it. That's not a recipe for success, and good earnings.

So, as dull as it may be, your aim is to keep your work environment well organized so that admin is a quick and painless activity. Here are some tips you may find useful:

- [ ] At the end of work each day, leave your desk clear. It takes just a few minutes to sort papers now, but a few hours if you leave them to pile up. And clutter isn't good for creativity.

- [ ] Invest in some ring-binders, lever-archs or box files, and file papers in different categories. For example, you may have one for finances, one for marketing, one for clients, and another for new business leads. Every time your financial year ends, create a folder for all your accounts and tax papers for that year.

- [ ] Have an in-tray where you dump all papers for the business and, once a week, spend some time going through it, dealing with the contents, throwing away what you don't need, and then filing the rest.

- [ ] Invest in a notice-board. Use it to organize your workload, and stick on info you need to access regularly, such as client phone numbers.

- [ ] Organize your stationery. Buy a desk tidy and bring some order to the bits and bobs lying about.

- [ ] Keep the paperwork for your current projects near to hand, separated into folders (clear plastic sleeves are ideal).

- [ ] Buy some storage boxes and archive old paperwork. You can keep the boxes close to hand in case you need to refer to an old file.

 Apply the same organizing principles to your computer. Separate files and emails into folders under different categories and archive off old ones you no longer need. Use desktop shortcuts to speed your access to files you open regularly.

Considering your comfort

You want your environment to support your working productively. The more comfortable you are, the less you think about your environment, and the more engrossed in work you can become.

Getting the temperature right

Think Goldilocks – not too hot, not too cold, just right. Too hot and you'll find yourself nodding off mid-afternoon; too cold and you'll struggle to focus. In winter, you may need a heater; in summer, a fan.

 Whenever you can, open the window. Fresh air invigorates the mind and stimulates creativity and productivity.

Reducing noise

When it comes to noise, everyone's different. You may like complete silence when you work, or prefer to work to music. Background noises like traffic, car alarms, workmen, and children playing may drive you insane, or you may find them a companionable hum.

 If, like Charlie, you fall into the 'make-a-noise-when-I'm-working-and-feel-my-wrath' camp, invest in some good-quality ear plugs and/or a white noise CD (sounds like waves or rain block out other noises).

Setting the light level

You've had your head down on a project all afternoon and finally you're done. You look up from your work and realize belatedly that it's dusk and the light has faded. No wonder your eyes itch and your head is aching.

Working in bad light is a common culprit for eye strain. Stick a high watt bulb in your overhead light, invest in a good work lamp, and, if possible, work in an area that has good natural light.

Being safety-conscious

When you work for yourself, there's no health and safety bloke to drone on about the dangers of staplers, or to drill into you that, in the event of a fire, you walk (not run) to the car park and assemble at point B. But this freedom from boring office procedures and rules doesn't mean you should completely forget about safety in your workplace.

Here are some safety basics:

☐ Don't overload power sockets. A four-gang adaptor leading from a four-gang adaptor is a recipe for fire.

☐ Fit a smoke alarm and keep a fire blanket and/or extinguisher in the house just in case.

☐ Keep the floor clear of trip hazards – cables, books, piles of proofs, slippery plastic wallets.

☐ Take care with hot drinks and food (and especially near IT equipment; Charlie has first-hand experience of what havoc a tuna pasta bake can wreak on a keyboard).

And, of course, remember what your teachers used to shout at you back in your schooldays: don't swing on your chair!

SUMMARY

✓ Plan your move into freelancing carefully, and only take the plunge when you're sure you can manage financially.

✓ Get your employment status straight: make sure you fall into the category of self-employed.

✓ Remember that as a sole trader you are your business – every penny you earn is yours, but you're also personally liable for any debt.

✓ Tell HMRC you're self-employed within three months of starting your business.

✓ Set up your Class 2 National insurance payments.

✓ Give plenty of thought to the business name you choose. Make it original, memorable, and simple.

✓ If possible, turn a room in your house into an office. If working in a communal room, section off your workspace.

✓ Set yourself up with a comfy, ergonomically-sound chair, a large desk, and room for storage.

✓ Get the right technology to do your job efficiently.

✓ Organize your office to minimize clutter.

✓ Make yourself comfortable: get the heat, noise, and light levels right.

✓ Be your own health and safety rep.

3

RUNNING YOUR BUSINESS

This chapter covers the nitty gritty of running your business – from laying down the law with clients to finding a happy, productive work style. It's in the daily activities of your business that you have the opportunity to be organized, efficient, professional, and sensible: attributes successful freelancers have by the bucketload.

It's beyond the scope of this book to take you through all the ins and outs of running a business. So instead, in this chapter we focus on the areas you most need to consider when freelancing in publishing.

PROTECTING YOURSELF WITH TERMS AND CONDITIONS

There's no obligation for a freelancer to lay down the terms and conditions for how they work. But if you want to avoid headaches with clients, it's wise to write some terms and conditions that apply to your freelancing, and then ask clients to read and accept them.

Looking at the benefits of terms and conditions

Yes, it's a hassle taking the time to come up with terms and conditions, but it's worth it in the long run. Here are some ways in which terms and conditions help you in business:

☐ **They can save you money.** Clients understand they can't get away with refusing to pay, paying less than they should, paying late, or not paying at all.

☐ **They help you avoid disagreements with clients.** Terms and conditions allow you to form a good, clear working relationship with clients because they know exactly where they are with you, and what to expect. If you clearly lay down your terms, no client can waste your time quibbling over your invoice, your deadline, or the work you produced to their brief.

☐ **They make you look professional.** Clients want to hire professional freelancers who clearly know how to run a business. Terms and conditions say, 'I'm a business person with experience and good sense, I'm in control, I'm assertive, and I know how to run my business.'

☐ **They help protect you from unfair treatment.** Not all clients operate in a fair, businesslike manner that's in keeping with your own preferences for working relationships. Clients are a lot less likely to take advantage of you if you come across as informed, assertive, and a consummate professional. And if a client who's agreed to your terms and conditions does cross the line, you're in a strong position to assert yourself.

Deciding on your terms and conditions

Here are some areas you may want to consider for your terms and conditions:

☐ **Costs:** Are costs such as telephone calls, printing, paper, CDs, and postage included in your project fee, or will you invoice these (at cost)? Does your client have the right to reduce the cost of your project fee for any reason? What happens if the client changes the brief mid-project, fails to meet deadlines, or terminates the project prematurely? Will you charge extra for out-of-hours or in-house work?

☐ **Deadlines:** In what circumstances will you have the right to alter an agreed deadline?

☐ **Invoicing and payment terms:** How and when will you invoice? How many days does the client have to pay? Will you require payment in instalments or upfront? What action will you take if the client pays late or doesn't pay at all?

☐ **Meetings and consultations:** Will you charge for meeting and consultation time, travel expenses, and/or travel time to attend a meeting? If so, how much?

☐ **Service definitions:** What exactly will you do for the client? What won't you do? What does your service involve?

You can also take a look at other freelancers' terms and conditions for inspiration and to get a feel for the wording.

Once you've set up your terms and conditions, ask new clients to agree to them before you commence work. You can do this by making your terms and conditions part of the project agreement, which we look into in a later section.

Agreeing to clients' terms and conditions

Corporate clients such as publishers often have their own terms and conditions to which you must agree before starting work.

Make sure you read a client's terms and conditions closely before signing on the dotted line, and that you abide by the agreement. For example, a client may well include a confidentiality clause in the terms and conditions that prohibits you from sharing information about the project.

If you have a problem with one of the client's terms and conditions, you'll need to decide whether to defer to the client's terms, or negotiate a change in the terms for this project. Realistically, though, it's very rare that a freelancer challenges a publisher over their terms. The publisher is king!

SETTING CLEAR BOUNDARIES: THE PROJECT AGREEMENT

The project agreement goes hand in hand with your terms and conditions. But whereas terms and conditions lay down the general dos and don'ts of working with you, the project agreement sets out the specific details and terms of a project.

The purpose of the project agreement is to clearly state the following:

☐ deadline
☐ fee
☐ nature of your service
☐ payment terms.

Opposite is an example project agreement to give you an idea of content.

By signing this document, a client is agreeing to both the specific project terms and your general terms and conditions.

Usually, project agreements are only necessary with private clients (authors) and small businesses. We don't give project agreements to publishers, because the publisher takes responsibility for laying down these terms (usually in a purchase order that you sign).

Since introducing project agreements and terms and conditions, we rarely have problems with clients. Most clients take on board the contents of these documents, and are a pleasure to work with. But you do come across the odd difficult client, and that's when you're glad you spent the time setting project terms.

BOOK WORK SERVICES
Project Quote

Client: Happy Day Publishing

Project: Book critique

Brief

Critique book in an overall document that covers characters, setting, plot, structure, writing style, title, length, readiness for publication and any further work required.

Deadline

Deadline is set at 11 a.m., Friday 10 July.

Cost

The project fee is £400.00.

Invoicing

The client must pay half the project fee (£200) upfront as security. The remainder (£200) will be payable within 14 days of submission of the completed critique.

I have read and agree to the terms in this document, together with the Book Work Services terms and conditions at www.bookworkservices.co.uk.

Signed:

Date:

Sarah Jones, 1 Hearth Road, Leicester, LE12 4RP

07777 123456

Take the case of Charlie's quibbling English teacher. This client hired Charlie to proofread his book (which, incidentally, was riddled with errors). This she did, to her usual high standards. However, after receiving the meticulously proofread text, the client told Charlie he wasn't happy with her service. Why? Because she hadn't done any rewriting to 'improve the flow' of the book (completely beyond the remit of a proofread). The client informed Charlie that, in view of her unsatisfactory service, he would only pay 50 per cent of her invoice.

Needless to say, Charlie was unimpressed. She had carried out the exact service the client had agreed to, and the client was at fault for misinterpreting the nature of a proofreading service. Happily, the client didn't have a leg to stand on with his completely unacceptable self-imposed discounting. Charlie referred the client to the project agreement he had signed. The project terms clearly indicated what her proofreading service entails (nothing to do with rewriting or flow), and her terms and conditions clearly state that the client has no right to reduce or refuse payment. Albeit with bad grace, the client was forced to admit his mistake and pay the full outstanding fee.

The moral of the story? Successful freelancers avoid getting drawn into unpleasant arguments with clients and ending up out of pocket by being prepared for the odd client who's out of line.

SIGNING CONFIDENTIALITY AGREEMENTS

It should be implicit in your role as a freelancer that you will respect the client's right to confidentiality. For example, on our blogs we may write something like, 'Today I'm working on a children's fantasy book', but we wouldn't dream of writing, 'Today I'm working on a children's book that's all about a talking dog called Pete and his adventures in a supermarket, for my client Steve Andrews'.

Usually, then, confidentiality is a matter of common sense. However, sometimes you come across a client who is particularly concerned about this area, and they may ask you to sign a confidentiality agreement. Ghostwriters in particular often have to sign to agree they won't disclose having worked on a book – that's why we can't shout about many of our published works.

The client usually supplies the agreement, but sometimes an author may ask you to do so. With a simple web search you can find a basic agreement that you can tailor for your needs.

UNDERSTANDING COPYRIGHT

When a freelancer creates a work (writing, art, design, and so on), they automatically own the copyright for that work. Strictly speaking, to ensure the copyright passes to the client, who of course wants to own the work, you need to sign it over in a contract. However, in the absence of a contract no court of law would uphold you claiming copyright infringement for a work you'd been commissioned to create that was being used as agreed. In these cases, the client that commissioned the work often has an 'implied licence' to use it.

Most freelancers are happy for their clients to take over the copyright of their work, and see it as an implicit part of their service. However, some freelancers – illustrators, for example – may want to limit the ways in which the client can use the material.

Publishers will cover copyright in a clause in the paperwork you sign; with authors you can draw up your own contract if required. We advise searching the web for example contracts you can adapt. If you're really concerned, you can seek advice from an intellectual property lawyer.

In reality, though, most freelancers don't worry about copyright because when they hand work over to a client, they're happy to relinquish their rights. That's the nature of the job.

SAFEGUARDING YOUR DATA

Two little words can avert disaster: back-up. As pessimistic as it sounds, never trust technology; it will always let you down sooner or later. Your computer will crash one day and, unless you're a computer whizz, whether you can recover your data or not is a matter of luck. Are you willing to stake your business's success on blind luck? Thought not!

The day Charlie's computer gave a sudden shuddering gasp and expired halfway through a job she was less than amused. Thankfully, the day before she'd safely backed up every last file and email, so her PC's untimely end didn't damage her business. She moved the back-up files onto her laptop, and her business transferred seamlessly over, so there was minimal down-time. This is exactly the kind of transition – planned for, simple, quick – you need to be able to make when (note we're not saying 'if') the IT Grim Reaper comes knocking.

There are various methods for backing-up:

☐ **CDs:** These are good for archiving old files you need to keep but won't use again.

☐ **External hard-drive:** Quick and easy back-ups for huge amounts of data.

☐ **Online:** You can pay a small fee to save a copy of your files with a secure online company.

- ☐ **Paper:** For important documents, such as key financial data for your tax return, it's wise to print a hard copy.

- ☐ **USB pens:** Inexpensive and quick.

- ☐ **Windows Home Server:** Designed for home computers to store data and back-up daily and automatically.

We recommend you get into the habit of backing-up your data once a week at the same time. That way, in the event of a computer meltdown, at worst you've only lost a week's data. Friday afternoons, when the weekend's approaching and your motivation for work subsides, is a good time to back-up.

Don't forget to save important emails as well. If you use Microsoft Outlook, you can set it up to export your emails to a file once a week.

 Keep a copy of your data off site. For example, once a month we send our husbands to work with a CD to be stored in their desks. That way, should disaster strike and our homes flood or burn down, we can salvage our businesses.

MANAGING YOUR WORKLOAD

Every freelancer develops their own work style. To be efficient and productive, you need to also be organized and strict with yourself.

Staying on top of work

Here's a golden rule for successful freelancing: never miss a deadline. You have to find a way to organize yourself so that you always deliver your work on time.

When you start a project, you can get paralyzed by the enormity of the job. The simplest way round this bottom-of-the-mountain-looking-up feeling is to break the task down into manageable chunks. So, break a book you're writing into chapters, and then into sections within a chapter. And say to yourself, 'Today I'll write two sections for Chapter 3', which feels a lot more manageable than, 'Today I'll start writing the book'.

Make sure you prioritize tasks effectively. Do the work with the closest deadline first. If you're bored with a particular job, mix and match with another, but always make sure you finish both jobs to deadline.

If you're struggling with a task – you have writer's block, for example – take a break and come back to it. Don't waste hours battling to continue and accomplishing little. Do some other work for a while, or go out for a walk to blow away the cobwebs.

 Don't let admin pile up while you focus on client work. Have an admin hour every week where you catch up on filing and tidying.

Working at the best times

Listen to your body clock. Are you an early bird or a night owl? Play to your strengths. If you work best in the morning and struggle to focus by late afternoon, try working from 7.30a.m. to 3.30p.m. If you're a grizzly bear in the morning but full of beans by evening you could work from 1p.m. to 8p.m. Or perhaps you like a power nap and a break mid-afternoon – try breaking your day into two shifts, say 9a.m. to 1p.m., then 3p.m. to 6p.m. By working during the hours your body is naturally more alert, you're more efficient.

Minimizing distractions

When working at home, shut yourself away and stick a 'Do Not

Disturb' sign on the door. Put in ear plugs or play music to block out background noise.

If you're trying to concentrate, turn off your phone (personal and work) for a while. The world won't end if people leave a message instead of speaking to you at once.

Also limit your email time. It's tempting to set your computer up to tell you whenever an email comes in, and to spend most of your day switching between emails and work. Unless you're dealing with an urgent email exchange, try to only look at emails every few hours. Set aside some time to deal with your messages, and then shut down the email program and get back to work without distractions.

KEEPING HAPPY, HEALTHY, AND PRODUCTIVE

For freelancers, work shouldn't be a daily grind. There's no Sunday night depression, no dragging yourself reluctantly into work, no watching the clock as it slowly, slowly ticks down the minutes until you can escape. Freelancing is about having things your way – fitting a job you love around your life, enjoying and being stimulated by your work, putting yourself first, and finding a happy balance in your life. With just a little know-how, you can keep happy, healthy, and productive – a recipe for successful freelancing.

Choosing interesting projects

Motivation really comes down to how interested you are in your work. From time to time, all freelancers do projects that don't particularly excite them, usually just to fill a gap or pay the bills. But, if possible, always ensure part of your workload consists of work you enjoy. And if you're struggling to find the enthusiasm to work on a boring project, break it into small chunks and mix and match fun projects with dreary ones.

Happy freelancing is all about finding balance. If you realize that you're spending a lot of your time unhappy in your work, you need to reassess the kinds of clients you're working with, or the types of projects you're doing.

Remember, you go freelance because you want to pick and choose your projects while doing something you're passionate about. If your workload isn't giving you the feelings of freedom and interest and challenge you want, you're the boss: make a change!

Learning to say 'no'

Freelancers can easily fall into the trap of letting their work take over their lives. The more hours you put in, the more you earn, so it's very tempting to say yes, yes, yes to all work offers. Every freelancer will have periods of working too hard, but you need to limit these times to keep a balance in your life.

Once you reach the point in your freelancing at which you can get by on your income, you can start thinking about how much more you want to take on. Life isn't just about working and earning as much as you possibly can. As difficult as you may find it, sometimes you have to turn a project down, or defer it, because you have enough on already or you need a break.

Alarm Bell

Pushing yourself too hard can lead to burnout. If you persistently bite off more than you can chew, you'll become exhausted and ill. You'll lose focus, forget important things like deadlines, and turn out shoddy work. So you'll damage your business – perhaps irrevocably. Saying no when you need to isn't a luxury, it's a necessity for success.

Dealing with isolation

If you work from home, chances are sometimes you get a bit lonely and suffer from cabin fever: feeling trapped and bored with your own company and the same four walls. This feeling can accumulate over the week and start to bring you down, detrimentally affecting your work efficiency.

Here are some ideas you can try for combating isolation.

☐ Chat with friends online during breaks in your work day.

☐ Get out and about in your free time – especially weekends.

☐ If you won't find it distracting, change the scene: take your work out into the garden, to your local library, or to a cafe.

☐ Join a gym, go swimming, or take an exercise class.

☐ Make friends with other freelancers who won't mind you emailing or phoning during work hours.

☐ Meet a friend for lunch now and again.

Make it a rule that you get out of the house every day, no matter how busy you are or what the weather's like. Fresh air and daylight are essential to keeping healthy, sleeping well, and having a sharp, creative mind. And just seeing other people while you're out and about makes you feel less lonesome and more connected to the world.

Taking plenty of breaks

Before we went freelance, we looked forward to taking breaks whenever we liked, and for as long as we liked, with no clock-watching boss keeping a beady eye on us. But we were rather surprised to discover this is far from how we work as freelancers. When we're busy, which we usually are, we can get lost in a project. With no distractions, it's easy to lose track of time as you steam through work. Then you suddenly realize you've been sitting at your desk for four hours solid, you're thirsty, you're hungry, you're cold, you're stiff, and you're in desperate need of a toilet break.

In the years we've been freelancing, we've had to learn to make ourselves stop for regular breaks. If we don't, we find we struggle with fatigue, and the quality of the work we produce suffers. Take a screen break a couple of times an hour – go to the toilet, make a cuppa, put some washing on – and take a proper half-hour break every four to five hours. During your longer breaks, do something completely different (don't read a novel if you've been editing all morning!) and, if possible, incorporate some activity – a walk, some stretches, yoga.

Switching off

When you work for yourself, especially at home, it can be very difficult to switch off from your work. Indeed, when you're settled on the sofa in the evening, watching a footie match, your projects can seem to call to you from your workspace, demanding your attention.

Ignore them! If you're confident that you're on top of your work (see the earlier section 'Managing your workload' for help with this), you need to allow yourself to walk away and have some wind-down time.

 If you find your head buzzes with work worries and ideas when you're 'off duty', keep a note pad at hand and empty your thoughts on to paper. Then promise yourself you'll deal with your notes when you're back 'on duty' again.

Protecting yourself from work-related illnesses

Working as a freelancer may not be particularly hazardous, compared to working as a firefighter or liontamer or skyscraper window cleaner, but that's not to say that your job doesn't have some health risks you should bear in mind:

- ☐ **Eye-sight:** Many freelancers spend hours every day staring at a visual display unit (VDU), and over time this can lead to damaged eyesight and headaches. Make sure you visit the optician for routine check-ups to keep an eye (excuse the pun) on the state of your sight.

- ☐ **Repetitive strain:** Typing and repeating actions with the mouse can result in repetitive strain injury (RSI): aches and pains in the hands, wrists, arms, neck, shoulders, or back. If this affects you, take plenty of breaks and see your GP if you can't shake off the pain.

- ☐ **Posture:** Those who work at a desk for long periods of time have a tendency to hunch over, causing a stiff neck and back. Invest in a supportive office chair, pay attention to your posture while seated, and take regular breaks to stretch out.

GOING IN-HOUSE

Some clients may ask you to work at their offices – either for a day or two or longer term. Some freelancers are happy to do this; others prefer to work solely from home.

Here are a few important questions to consider before agreeing to freelance in-house:

☐ Will the client reimburse travel expenses? And are you happy to lose part of your working day to travel?

☐ Why does the client want you to work in-house? Is it actually necessary for you to go to the client, or could you work at home and over the phone?

☐ How will you manage your other clients/projects? For example, can you check emails at the client's office and respond to other clients?

☐ How do you feel about being part of a team, but an outsider still?

☐ How will you manage working in front of a client? Will you have to alter your work style?

We prefer to work from home – we like our own space and we're far too lazy to get up at the crack of dawn, put on a suit, and join the throngs on public transport to commute to a publishing house. But when she was first starting out as a freelancer, Charlie did undertake the odd in-house stint, as a way to build experience and, of course, earn some extra money. She soon discovered she wasn't at ease working in an office environment again, and in several placements she found the work pace agonizingly slow (imagine being hired for seven days to do a job that would take you three at home – yawn!).

However, each to their own – please don't be put off by our reluctance to work in-house, because that's simply our personal choice. We know freelancers who love blending in-house work with home-working, because then they get the best of both worlds. Working at home all week can get pretty boring and lonely, so the odd trip into town can add some much-needed variety and stimulation.

Alarm Bell

Working in-house for one client for a long time can alter your status from self-employed freelancer to employee of the organization. See Chapter 2 for more.

EVOLVING YOUR BUSINESS

The beauty of freelancing is that you're free to move your business in any direction you choose. Be open to change and your freelancing can take you places you never imagined.

Increasing your rates

As you gain experience, you may decide to raise your rates to reflect your expertise and background. Over time, rates in the industry also naturally rise with inflation. So, if you've been charging the same for a couple of years, it's probably time to review your rates.

Your best bet for working out whether you should up your rates is to check out what other freelancers are charging (see Chapter 7).

Developing your services

It's important not to set your business in stone but instead to be willing to embrace change. Many freelancer businesses evolve over time, directed by the freelancer's experiences, desires, and passions. What you do at the start of your freelancing career may shape your future work, but it doesn't have to dictate it.

For example, Charlie started out offering freelance marketing copywriting, proofreading, and editing. She did some work for publishers, but most of her clients were corporate. Over time, she added book critiquing as a service, then book writing, then book development services, then ghostwriting. Finding that she most enjoyed her editorial and book-related projects, Charlie decided to drop copywriting altogether. For a while, she focused exclusively on books, working with authors and publishers, and then she added back her editorial services for businesses, to broaden her client base in a struggling economy. Looking to the future, Charlie fully expects her business to keep evolving in this way; she knows that being open to change, and keeping a close eye on what's working and what isn't, is essential to maintain a solid client base (see Chapter 8 for more on keeping clients happy).

As well as adding new services, dropping ones you dislike, and developing existing ones, freelancing also gives you the opportunity to do something completely different as well. If it takes your fancy, you can set up another business alongside your freelancing – selling stuff on eBay, gardening, teaching kick-boxing. For example, we know a very successful freelancer who works both as an animator and also a photographer, and thoroughly enjoys doing both.

Considering outsourcing

Some freelancers develop their businesses to the point that they consider setting up an agency of sorts and outsourcing work to others. For example, you may be a book indexer who always has more work than you can handle, so you decide to set up a book indexing business, doing some work yourself and hiring others to do the rest.

Outsourcing is the freelancer's equivalent of a company taking on staff. Say a client is willing to pay £300 for a book index. You may pay another freelancer £250 to do the work, and then invoice the client £300, so making £50.

On the surface, outsourcing can look like a way to take advantage of other freelancers – how can it be fair to pay them less than you receive? But many freelancers are happy to be subcontracted. Those new to freelancing can't command the highest rates, and want to gain experience. And many freelancers are happy to pay the 'agency' a cut for passing them the work. As long as the subcontracted freelancers' rates are reasonable, this practice is perfectly acceptable in the business world.

Before you consider outsourcing work, bear in mind the following:

- ☐ **You must be upfront with clients.** We once met a freelancer who subcontracted projects without the author's or publisher's knowledge. This is dishonest, and very risky. If you're discovered, you can expect a very angry client who probably won't pay, will refuse to hire you again, and may bad-mouth you to others in the industry (and rightly so).

- ☐ **You'll be responsible for the work you hand over to clients – whether you did it or not.** So, if another freelancer takes on a project for you, you either have to trust that person implicitly or check their work yourself before passing it to the client. And if you end up spending a lot of time checking other freelancers' work, it rather defeats the object of not doing the work yourself!

- ☐ **You must have the cash to pay the freelancers you hire.** Say you subcontract three jobs from authors in a month – editing jobs worth £500, £300, and £150. Your freelancers want payment within 14 days. That means you have to come up with £950 to pay your freelancers even if the authors haven't paid you yet. It's simply unfair to leave the freelancers unpaid until the authors pay: you are the freelancers' client and you must pay their invoices on time.

- ☐ **You'll be a manager.** Subcontracting means managing other people – being the spider in the web who organizes the project. You'll have to spend time on boring admin tasks and you'll have to keep on top of your freelancers' deadlines. This is time you won't spend doing your own projects, which may mean over time you become more of a project manager than a writer or illustrator or book reviewer or whatever.

We advise you to think very closely before moving from freelancing to managing an agency. In our experience, clients prefer to work directly with an individual rather than a business. Publishers, in particular, tend to avoid agencies.

TAKING TIME OFF

One of the most attractive things about freelancing is that you're free to take time out of work whenever you like. There's no pesky holiday allowance, no boss on your case because you've taken a duvet day, no worries about job security if you decide to take a sabbatical and trek around the world for three months.

However, if you want to maintain a solid client base and earn a decent income, you do need to be sensible and professional about time off. You need to communicate clearly and in a timely manner with clients, especially where your time off will affect a project.

Alarm Bell

Never take on a project when you know you'll be away at a crucial time or may not be able to meet the deadline.

Longer periods of leave require expert handling. Maternity and paternity leave is a good example that affects many freelancers. Lengthy parental leave can see you out of business for months, and if you don't want to return to a lack of clients and projects (and therefore money), you need to plan to keep your business on the back burner rather than dead and buried. Here are some tips born out of our experience with maternity leave:

□ Inform clients in advance of your upcoming leave. How early you tell clients depends on the projects you have on and how you work with a client (if the client only hires you now and again, there's no rush; but if it's a major, regular client you need to give warning).

☐ Give clients an idea of when you intend to return to work, and reassure them that you're looking forward to working with them again soon.

☐ Place a message on your website explaining your leave, and set an out-of-office message on your email auto-responder inviting clients to get in touch when you're back to work (provide a date).

☐ A couple of months before the end of your leave, notify clients when you'll be returning to work.

☐ A week or so before you start work, get in touch with clients and ask to be kept in mind for projects.

If you've told a client you're taking paternity or maternity leave, when you return to work ensure you convey to clients that you're still a serious, professional freelancer who's committed to their job. A client will not want to work with someone who comes across as being distracted by parenthood. Don't answer the phone to a client with a crying baby in your arms; don't start every email with toddler Harry's latest clever trick; and don't give clients the impression that you're juggling parenthood and work to the point of typing with one hand and burping a baby with the other.

SUMMARY

✓ Set terms and conditions for your business and seek clients' agreement.

✓ Issue clients with project agreements.

✓ Draw up a copyright contract if you feel it is necessary.

✓ Back-up your data religiously.

✓ Always meet deadlines.

✓ Break tasks down into manageable chunks.

✓ Choose your working hours to suit your body clock.

✓ Resist the temptation to check emails all day.

✓ Look for projects that you'll enjoy.

✓ Set a limit on how much work you take on.

✓ Get out of the house every day.

✓ Take regular breaks.

✓ Be open to change and ready to evolve your business.

✓ Plan time out carefully and be sure to communicate effectively with clients to minimize loss of income.

4

MONEY, MONEY, MONEY

The bottom line is this: you're in business to make money. You may be a freelance illustrator or writer or researcher because you genuinely love your work, but we doubt very much you'd do it for nothing.

Money, then, is everything, and to succeed in freelancing you need to get good at managing the financial side of your business. You need to charge rates that are competitive but bring in a good income. You need to be professional in running your accounts – invoicing clients and logging expenses. You need to be assertive in chasing up unpaid invoices. You need to handle your taxes accurately, or else pay someone else to do so. And you need to get on top of your tax bills and budget for them in advance.

Sounds complicated? Don't worry; by the end of this chapter you'll be reaching for your calculator with confidence.

SETTING YOUR RATES

The subject of rates is the one we're most commonly asked about. Your success as a freelancer depends on your ability to earn a good wage for what you do. Freelancers need to know what to charge, and what to base their rates on. We have to be competitive, but make sure we're earning a decent income.

The following sections take you through what you need to consider when setting your rates.

Steering clear of ridiculous rates

A big problem in the publishing industry is freelancers working for silly money. As long as there are freelancers prepared to work for low hourly rates, publishers will be reluctant to pay much more appropriate ones.

Ultimately, rates increase in line with experience. However, that doesn't mean you should work for insultingly low fees at the start of your freelancing career.

When thinking about fees, bear in mind that freelancers should earn a better hourly rate than those who work in-house because they have no benefits (sick leave, pension, paid holidays), they have overheads (for example, electricity bills), and they have to cover the natural ebb and flow of their work.

Remember also that freelancers are skilled professionals, and should be paid as such. Take proofreaders, for example. There are many people out there who think they can proofread, but in fact trained professionals are an elite group – they're experts in their field and will spot many errors that the average chap on the street will not.

If you charge very low fees, you may find it easy to get work. But think of the large volume of work you'll have to do in order to make ends meet! A freelancer who earns £20 per hour can work half as many hours as a freelancer who earns £10 and still earn the same amount.

Charging reasonable, competitive rates sends a clear signal to your clients that you have a good knowledge of the industry and your competition, and your services match the quality of the amount you charge. When deciding between hiring a £9-per-hour illustrator or a £25-per-hour one, which do you think the client will assume is the better, more professional illustrator?

If a client is quibbling with your reasonable rates, and telling you they know another freelancer who'll do the job for a much lower fee, we advise you to tell that client to go ahead and hire the cheap freelancer. A business-savvy client would realize that if you pay peanuts, you get monkeys. Don't work for people who refuse to pay you what you're worth!

Deciding what to charge by

You have four choices for how to charge:

- ☐ **By the day:** You set a daily rate. For example, you may charge rewriting a book as seven days' work.

- ☐ **By the hour:** You set an hourly rate. For example, you may charge writing a press release as three hours' work.

- ☐ **By the project:** You offer a flat fee for the project. For example, you may charge £15,000 for ghostwriting a 60,000 word book.

- ☐ **By the unit:** You charge per 1,000 words for proofreading, critiquing, editing, or writing, or per picture for illustration. For example, you may charge £10 per 1,000 words to copy-edit a book.

You may stick to one of these styles of costing, or you may mix and match depending on the client and the project.

Coming up with initial rates

When you first go freelance, you may be fumbling in the dark for a bit with rates. Here are some tips to help you decide your initial rates:

- ☐ Check out the competition and match your rates accordingly (see Chapter 7).

☐ If you have any freelancer friends or contacts in publishing houses, ask for advice.

☐ Use recommended minimum rates, such as those issued by the Society for Editors and Proofreaders (www.sfep.org.uk) and the National Union of Journalists (www.londonfreelance.org/fees guide) as a guideline.

Also consider your basic living costs. How much money do you need to make each month to survive? Divide the monthly sum down into a minimum daily rate, and you have a baseline for your rates.

Always add a little to your costing as a contingency for going over time on a project.

Getting good at estimating time

As you gain experience in freelancing, you'll get better at assessing how long it will take you to complete a project, which means you'll get better at working out a decent fee.

If you really want to get a clear picture of how you're doing with your costings, try keeping a project log. Keep a running tally of the total time you spend on a project and, after the project, enter details like time taken and cost into a spreadsheet.

Opposite is an example project log for Bob, a fictional proofreader.

This log helps Bob determine that, on average, he reads 4,500 words per hour. He can use this figure to calculate a reasonable fee for a book where he knows the word count. The log also helps Bob see where he charged too little (Book 6) and where he charged wisely (Book 5). This knowledge can inform future rate-setting.

Project	Total hrs	Total wds	Wds p/hr	Total pay	Pay p/ 1,000 wds	Pay per hr
Book 1	8.75	35,000	4,000	175	5.00	20
Book 2	10	50,000	5,000	220	4.40	22
Book 3	18	81,000	4,500	300	3.70	18
Book 4	21	84,000	4,000	250	2.97	19
Book 5	25	100,000	4,000	580	5.80	25
Book 6	19	95,000	5,000	247	2.60	13

Adapting your rates from project to project

There's a good reason why we don't advertise our rates on our websites: each project is unique. We don't have static rates; we have cost brackets we charge within, and we charge whatever suits a particular project.

Here are some factors that affect your rates:

☐ **Depth of work involved:** You charge less for proofreading a well-written book that only has the odd typo than one that's riddled with mistakes.

☐ **Timescale:** If the client wants a quick turnaround, you may charge more. Charlie offers an express service for an extra 25 per cent that's popular with clients who are against the clock (it's amazing how an author who's spent a year writing their book can suddenly decide it must be edited now, now, now!).

☐ **Type of work:** Editing costs more than proofreading, writing costs more than editing, colour drawings cost more than line sketches, and so on.

In order to glean this information, you need to get a very clear brief from the client before you decide on a rate. In addition, if applicable, you need to see a sample of the material the client wants you to work on.

Learning from your mistakes

Every freelancer gets it wrong sometimes when it comes to rates. Occasionally this is a happy error: you predict a project will take more time than it does, so make brilliant money for the hours you put in. But sometimes you reckon a project will take you three days and it takes five, so your hourly rate takes a hammering.

If a project is taking longer than anticipated, don't think you can run to the client for more money. When you agree a costing with a client, it's completely unprofessional not to honour your agreed price. If you've made a mistake in the costing, you have to accept that and get on with the work regardless. Only if a client is moving goalposts or demanding more work could you request further payment, and this will be covered in your project agreement and terms and conditions of work (see Chapter 3).

When you complete a project and realize you've made less money than anticipated, try not to get too disheartened. The more you freelance, the less this will happen as you gain experience and learn from your mistakes. Soon it will be the norm that you're happy with the totals on the invoices you send to clients.

CHARGING CLIENTS

Every time you charge a client for your services, you need to give your client an invoice, and keep a copy for your records.

The invoice includes:

- a summary of the services you're invoicing for
- the client's name and address
- the client's purchase order number for the job, if applicable
- the date

- ☐ the invoice number (this is for your record-keeping)
- ☐ the payment terms (how quickly the client must pay)
- ☐ the total amount you're charging (this may be broken down into parts)
- ☐ your business name, if applicable
- ☐ your name and address.

Here's an example:

BOOK WORK SERVICES

Happy Day Publishing
17 Sunny Lane
Oxford
OX3 2RJ
16 January 2010

INVOICE NO: 712

DESCRIPTION	AMOUNT
Proofreading *1001 Reasons to Be Happy*	£450.00
Postage of proofs	£10.00
TOTAL	£460.00

Please pay within 14 days. I reserve the right to charge interest should payment be later than 30 days from the date on this invoice.

Thank you,

Sarah Jones

1 Hearth Road, Leicester, LE12 4RP ~ 07777 123456

Most clients expect you to email invoices, but some still require you to send them by snail mail. Issue the invoice on the day you return the completed work to the client.

 Print invoices and keep them in a file. Then, if your computer ever dies, you have a paper copy back-up.

You may decide to split payment down into two or more invoices. This may be for a number of reasons:

- ☐ You haven't worked for a client before and you want them to pay you half the project fee upfront as security. We only advise doing this for very small businesses and private authors because it's not usual business practice.

- ☐ The project is large and time-consuming, and to help your cash flow you want to be paid by instalments. For example, if you're writing a book it will take you several months, and you probably can't afford to wait for a fat cheque at the end of the project.

- ☐ Your client requests instalment payments. This can be a way of securing business where your client may not otherwise have been able to hire you. Authors, in particular, don't always have the cash ready for a big project.

Your client should have no reason to quibble the invoice amount, because they agreed the cost of your service in advance (see Chapter 3 for more on project agreements).

You also need to consider how you'll ask clients to pay you. Here are your options:

- ☐ **Bank transfer:** This is a very quick, easy way to receive payment, but do be aware of bank charges. Some freelancers prefer not to give out their bank details.

☐ **Cash:** Few clients pay this way; it's inconvenient and can seem unprofessional.

☐ **Cheque:** You have to take the time to bank it, and there's a delay on monies transferring, but it's secure.

☐ **PayPal:** This is becoming increasingly popular with private clients, because it's secure and fast, but don't expect publishers to use this method!

GETTING PAID ON TIME

The new freelancer can find it a bit of a shock to discover that clients don't always pay up promptly. Some take weeks, months even to pay you. And, even more maddeningly, you get the odd one or two who try not paying at all.

When we first went freelance, we found payment timing to be a huge problem. Often, we were surviving on beans on toast because we hadn't made enough money; we'd earned the money but hadn't been paid. Pretty soon we had to toughen up with clients. Successful freelancers don't put up with being out of pocket. They must behave as any other business and instigate professional credit control procedures.

Avoiding late and non-payment

Clients are often lovely people to work with during a project, but bringing up the subject of money can create an awkward atmosphere in your working relationship. You want to protect your client base; therefore, as far as possible you want to avoid getting to the stage where you have to get tough with a client over money.

You need to ensure your clients understand exactly when you expect payment. Whatever your payment terms (for example, 14 days), you need to communicate them to clients very clearly, so they know by when they must pay. Include your payment terms in your terms and conditions and project agreements (see Chapter 3), and on your invoice.

Also make it clear to clients that you take credit control seriously. Charlie adds this sentence to her invoices: 'I understand and will exercise my statutory right to claim interest and compensation for debt recovery costs under the late payment legislation should payment be later than 14 days from the date on this invoice' (this is a government-recommended addition to an invoice). One recent client was so impressed by Charlie's invoice he paid within an hour of receiving it; now that's our kind of client!

Showing clients you mean business

You either agree a credit period with your client (for example, 14 days), or the law sets a default period of 30 days. If an invoice is not paid within the credit period, it becomes overdue.

 Create a 'payments outstanding' spreadsheet. Log all invoices you send out, and their due date for payment. When an invoice is paid, remove it from the list. When you notice one is unpaid and has gone over the due date, chase it up.

Start by sending a friendly reminder by email, then progress to more formal emails and a polite phone call. Keep your tone professional, but firm. And keep a record of all communications.

If your invoice is more than two months overdue and you're getting nowhere chasing payment – you're being ignored or your client is saying yes, yes but still doing nothing – you may need to step things up a gear. By law, you are entitled to charge the client debt recovery costs and interest on the unpaid invoice (Business Link's website explains this), and if you have exhausted all other avenues you can take a client to court. Often, just informing clients that you'll pursue these options is enough to get them signing a cheque.

Alarm Bell

Think very carefully before getting heavy with clients. If you charge interest and debt recovery costs, or you take the client to court, you're unlikely to work with them again, and the client could bad-mouth you and attempt to destroy your reputation. These are serious actions that you should not take lightly.

Sick of chasing, some freelancers write off debts. Not Charlie! Despite repeated phone calls, emails and letters, Company X was three months overdue paying a £3,000 invoice. The client – the owner of a small business – had tried every excuse in the book: 'I'll pay you next week', 'The cheque's in the post', 'I'm waiting to be paid by one of my clients'. Finally, when she received a payment cheque and it bounced, Charlie called in the big boys: a local debt collection agency. The agency immediately began court proceedings, and visited the client's premises to assess which goods of value they might be able to seize. The visit gave the client a real fright, but he still didn't pay up. It became clear that his business was in difficulties and he was fighting creditors off with a stick. Eventually, the court issued a County Court Judgment in Charlie's favour, ordering Company X to pay the outstanding invoice together with a few hundred pounds that covered debt recovery costs and interest. And she was just in time: soon after, the company went bust.

DEDUCTING BUSINESS EXPENSES

As with any other business, freelancers deduct the cost of business-related expenses from their turnover (the money they receive from clients) to determine their profits (actual income). The lower your income, the less tax you pay. So, the more business expenses you offset against your income, the less tax you pay overall.

Business expenses, then, sound like a great opportunity to save money. But this is where freelancers must tread very, very carefully. HMRC have some strict rules for what you can and can't claim as a business expense, and – tempting as it may be – shoving costs that don't strictly relate to your work through your books can land you in hot water with the tax authorities.

Here's an idea of the kind of things you can claim for:

- ☐ hosting fee for your website
- ☐ new computer (but a proportion only because you won't use it solely for business)
- ☐ postage stamps for a mailshot
- ☐ train journey to meet a client.

Here are some examples of things you can't claim for:

- ☐ CDs to listen to while you work
- ☐ lunch you bought for a client
- ☐ new suit to wear to business meetings
- ☐ parking ticket incurred while visiting a client.

If you hire an accountant, they will tell you what receipts to hand over for your accounts. If you do your own books, you'll need to educate yourself fully on what you can legally claim (see the later section 'Finding help' for resources you can use).

Remember to keep hold of all receipts for your expenses. By law you must keep all your financial records and paperwork for five years, in case HMRC want to see them. Back-up electronic files (see Chapter 3) and put paperwork in a safe place.

 TOP TIP Each month, spend a couple of hours logging your expenses on a spreadsheet alongside the invoices you sent out. Then you can set the spreadsheet up so that it calculates your profits, and even estimates what tax you owe.

FILING YOUR TAX RETURN

You have two options when it comes to your tax return: pay an accountant or tackle it yourself. It really comes down to personal preference and your individual circumstance. Emma, for example, prefers to pay an accountant to take the stress out of tax return time; Charlie taught herself the basics of tax and files her own.

Hiring an accountant

Self-employed freelancers aren't legally obliged to hire an accountant. HMRC's self-assessment system is designed to allow people to handle their own finances (hence 'self-assessment'), but some people hate the idea of managing accounts and filling in tax returns. The responsibility feels huge, the sums too complicated, the entire exercise dull, dull, dull.

Hiring an accountant is great because:

☐ The accountant does all the work – you either hand over your invoices and receipts or an overall log of both.

☐ You don't have to worry about errors in your tax return that can get you in trouble with the tax authorities.

☐ Your accountant may find ways to reduce your tax bill, saving you more than the cost of their services.

Alarm Bell

Notice the use of the word 'may' in the final bullet point – although your accountant *may* save you money, it's not guaranteed. You may end up paying upwards of £200 per year simply for the luxury of having someone else fill in a form for you. If you're only using an accountant's services to cut your costs, make sure you get proof that they will actually do this. Charlie once went to an accountant with a view to hiring him, and asked him how much money he would save her. The answer was a big fat zero. Because Charlie's financial affairs were straightforward, it turned out she was doing just fine handling her own accounts.

In some cases it's essential to seek the advice of an accountant or tax adviser:

☐ If your income is approaching the higher tax band (over £37,400 at the time of writing), in which case an accountant may be able to save you tax.

☐ If you're approaching the threshold for registering for VAT (£68,000 at the time of writing).

☐ If your tax affairs are complicated; for example, you have two or more jobs, you're a landlord, or you have investments.

You should also consider finding an accountant if you're really struggling with your book-keeping, or it's getting you down. There's no shame in having an accountant. In fact, you could argue that your time is much better spent doing the client work you excel at than fumbling about with spreadsheets and tax calculations.

Whether you choose to hire an accountant or not, be organized in your record-keeping. Even if an accountant takes care of your tax return, keep a clear picture of payments in and out of your business. That way, you can keep track of your profits and estimate your tax, which allows you to budget for tax bills. And organize your records; hand your accountant a shoebox stuffed with receipts and scrummed-up invoices and their fee may increase.

Handling the return yourself

If you want to save a couple of hundred pounds a year on an accountant's fee, you can do your own tax return. In order to do your own return you need to:

- [ ] be able to do basic maths, such as calculating percentages
- [ ] be willing to take responsibility for the accuracy of your return
- [ ] have fairly simple financial affairs
- [ ] understand basic tax law and how to fill in the tax return (you can learn this).

Tax returns aren't actually as scary as you may think. There's plenty of help available and, for freelancers, the return is fairly straightforward – a case of noting down money in and out. And if you file your tax return online (which we strongly recommend), you have plenty of time to work on the form before you submit it, and when you press 'submit' the system automatically calculates your bill.

Although you have until 31 January to submit your tax return online, try to do it much earlier in the year – say May or June. That way, when the online calculator tells you the exact total of your tax bill for the following January, you have plenty of time to ensure you can afford that bill.

If you file your own tax return, then you are responsible for the accuracy of the information you provide. Don't let this terrify you: HMRC are understanding about genuine mistakes. However, don't think you can get away with being dishonest on your return. HMRC have beady eyes, and they keep a close eye on people whose tax bills are microscopic. Plus, every year HMRC look into the finances of a sample of people chosen at random. You could easily be on the list.

PAYING YOUR TAXES

As Benjamin Franklin famously put it, 'In this world nothing can be said to be certain, except death and taxes'. Like it or not, you're going to have to give a proportion of your hard-earned dough to the government each year.

Freelancers pay two tax bills each year: the first by 31 January and the second by 31 July. It's important to pay your bills on time to avoid a £100 fine.

No one likes bills, especially those that they can't afford. Coming up with a few extra quid for an unexpectedly high gas bill isn't likely to be a problem, but needing to find a few thousand to pay your tax bill is disastrous. The only way to cope with tax bills is to set aside plenty of money in readiness.

We recommend you follow the basic rule of setting a third of your income aside for tax. This ensures your tax bills are covered, and you may even have some surplus.

 Every time a client pays you, move a third into an ISA or high-interest savings account. You're less likely to spend the money then, and by the time you come to pay your tax bill you'll have earned some decent interest.

Alarm Bell

It can be tempting to dip into the wodge of money you're keeping in the bank. You think, *I'll use that lump sum to pay off my wedding now, and then earn it back later.* This is risky. What if work slows and you struggle to put back the money you've essentially borrowed from HMRC? Don't use your tax fund as a useful cash-flow facility.

OPENING A BUSINESS BANK ACCOUNT

There's no legal obligation for a sole trader to run their business finances through a business bank account. As long as you keep your personal bank statements and can highlight which incoming and outgoing payments relate to your work, HMRC are happy.

However, your bank may not be. Money-grabbers that they are, banks like self-employed people to set up separate bank accounts. Why? You guessed it – because these accounts come with higher fees and penalties.

If you only have a few clients, you may be able to get away with putting client payments into a personal account. However, if a steady stream of payments is coming into your personal account, your bank may take notice and request (demand) you switch to a business account.

Business accounts do have some advantages:

- ☐ They make you look professional. For example, clients can write a cheque out to your business name (if you use one).

- ☐ They separate your business income and expenditure, making it easier to see how your business finances are going.

- ☐ They provide some security – you aren't sharing your personal bank details.

But the drawback of business bank accounts is that they can be costly. Some charge monthly fees for the account; others find cunning ways to sting you, such as charging fees for paying in cheques or withdrawing money.

Charlie was once furious to discover her bank had taken a percentage of a payment from a client who'd settled his invoice by paying cash directly into her account at a branch. No client had ever paid in this manner before, so she hadn't realized a fee would apply. What a waste of £40, when her client could easily have sent a cheque instead! And to top it all off, the bank charge had been applied on a day the balance in her account was zero, so she became overdrawn. And then, of course, she had to pay an overdraft fee as well. Infuriating! But really, she had no one to blame but herself because she should have read the smallprint for the account more closely.

If you do open a business bank account, rather than emptying it each time you get paid, leave a float in the account – say £50 or £100. That way, you've covered any unexpected fees, and you also have money in the account for business expenses, such as a train fare or stationery shop.

FINDING HELP

Many freelancers find financial matters daunting. After all, we're creatives at heart, not mathematicians. If you're finding your accounts unaccountably tricky and your tax return decidedly taxing, don't panic; support is available.

Accountants and tax advisers

An hour with a financial whizz may help you get your head around a particular aspect of finance that's confusing you. You can pay for a consultation, or be very cheeky and chat to one with a view to hiring them (most accountants offer a free initial consultation) and then use the information provided for yourself.

Business Link

This is the government's business support organization, and it offers free advice to self-employed people.

- ☐ **Helpline (0845 600 9 006):** If you prefer to chat to someone.

- ☐ **Website (www.businesslink.gov.uk):** Full of useful info and very user-friendly.

Directgov

The Directgov website (www.direct.gov.uk) gives you access to a range of information and services from the government. It includes information on self-employment and self-assessment that we find is more accessible than HMRC text.

HMRC

HMRC have a duty to help you with your tax affairs. However, be aware that, in our opinion, they aren't always very good at simplifying concepts for the novice freelancer!

- ☐ **Website (www.hmrc.gov.uk):** Contains a wealth of information on taxation and filling in your tax return. Some of the info is easy to grasp; other pages are pretty technical.

☐ **Helplines:** HMRC also have various helplines to guide you through aspects of self-assessment, national insurance, income tax, VAT, and tax returns. For a full listing of helpline numbers, go to 'Contact us' on the HMRC website and select 'self-employed'.

☐ **Local branch:** HMRC have local offices that handle enquiries and they sometimes offer local training courses – Charlie once attended a very useful one on filling in her tax return.

Google

The internet is a rich source of all kinds of information, and a simple web search using an engine like Google can get you the answers you need. For example, if you want to know what business expenses you can legally claim, a web search will offer plenty of information from the government, financial advice websites, and accountancy firms.

SUMMARY

✓ Don't fall into the trap of charging rates that fall well below the industry standard in an attempt to get work. Only monkeys charge peanuts.

✓ Keep your eye on recommended minimum rates for publishing freelancers.

✓ Record project details in a log to help you get a clear picture of what to charge.

✓ Don't feel you need to have set fees; be flexible and adapt according to each project.

✓ Issue an invoice to a client when requesting payment, and split fees down into instalments if necessary.

✓ Clearly communicate to clients your payment terms.

✓ Keep track of payments outstanding and chase clients when invoices become overdue.

✓ Understand which business expenses you can claim, and which you can't.

✓ Hire an accountant if you don't want to take charge of your tax return, but make sure they offer value for money.

✓ If you file your own tax return make sure you thoroughly research how to do this.

✓ Put money aside as you earn, ready for tax bills.

✓ Pay attention to the small print of business bank accounts.

✓ Ask for help if you're struggling with the financial side of running a business; don't soldier on alone and make costly mistakes.

5

MARKETING YOUR BUSINESS

So you've set up shop and are ready to start your new life as a freelancer, yet the phone isn't exactly ringing off the hook, and your bank statement is looking pretty bleak. The problem is that *you* know that you're ready to get stuck in, but nobody else does.

Often, we can get so caught up in the excitement of actually setting up the business that we forget all about letting others know we exist. Emma spent weeks choosing the right PC, sorting out her admin, and rearranging her pencil box when, quite honestly, she could have paid a bit more attention to advertising her services.

This can be one of the trickiest parts of starting a new business – spreading the word and getting your name out there in order to attract prospective clients. That's why marketing both you and your business is crucial in order to be a success.

DEFINING YOUR MARKETING STRATEGY

With every new business comes a requirement for a clearly defined marketing strategy. So what is marketing? Well, it's essentially a way of promoting yourself and your services to a target client base.

 When it comes to setting out your own marketing plan, begin by asking yourself four main questions:

☐ Who are your potential clients?
☐ What area of the market do you want to focus on?

☐ What can you do to get your target client to give you their business?

☐ How much can you afford to spend on marketing?

This is where extensive research comes in handy. Research will help you to identify your competitors, see what they're up to (and what you can do better), and find your own target market. The research process will also help you in building a list of potential clients you can contact. For example, if you're promoting yourself as a copy editor and proofreader, then pick up a copy of the *Writers' & Artists' Yearbook* (or the Bible, as it is sometimes known in publishing circles). Then go through all the publishers listed and make a note of those that would most require the services you have to offer. Then think about how you're going to approach them.

 Consider your existing network too. What contacts do you have that might be interested in your skills?

It's also useful to make a marketing budget and figure out how much you want to invest in promoting your business. Although placing advertisements in trade publications can be useful, it can be a costly exercise, and one you might want to postpone until the real money starts flowing in. However, for the budget-conscious freelancer, there are plenty of more affordable ways to spread the word about your business.

REPRESENTING YOUR BUSINESS

Business cards are essential to any new business. They send the message that you're professional and take your own business seriously. After all, which is better – scribbling your name and number on a hastily torn-off piece of paper, or handing over a clean, crisp business card that tells the interested party exactly what you do, and how you can be contacted?

These days, business cards don't need to cost the earth and there are plenty of companies on the internet that will provide a set of 50 or 100 cards for very little money. You can even design your own, by choosing from a selection of patterns or creating your own image to make your card unique.

It's easy to get carried away when designing your own card, so just remember to keep it clean and simple. Those with too much information on them tend to put off the recipient, and will rarely be taken seriously.

Emma made a bit of a mess with her first experimentation with business cards, and frankly took far too long over them. She discovered a 'business cards for simpletons' sort of website that suited her down to the ground, and spent days choosing the perfect design to represent herself and her burgeoning business. Eventually (and having annoyed everyone else around her getting feedback), she chose a lovely, peaceful, calm sunset design, which, in hindsight, would have been more appropriate for an aromatherapy business.

Next, she thought of a slogan that would really capture the essence of what her business was all about, so she came up with 'Tailored services designed to suit your deadlines', which wasn't exactly genius given the amount of time she spent over it. Then she thought about the services she would offer, and the more she thought about it, the more services she came up with. Of course, she could provide editing, copy-editing, proofreading, ghostwriting, copywriting, transcribing, typesetting, and website building services, couldn't she? There was simply not enough room on the back of that business card to fit in all her God-given talents, but she crammed them all in anyway.

However, worst of all, when she presented her crisp, brand-new card to an editor at a major publishing house, she looked at it and was singularly unimpressed. Apparently, Emma had made the rookie mistake of listing too many services on the back of the card. 'There's only one of you, and yet you claim to do anything and everything. This card says that you have too many balls in the air and you lack the focus to really commit to one area. Clients will think you're not putting enough time and energy into the projects that they've assigned you, and this will concern them.'

Obviously, Emma was a bit disappointed; what a waste of good business cards! But she was grateful for an expert's feedback and ended up narrowing down the list to three main services: ghostwriting, editing, and copywriting. In a way, it was a very useful exercise as it helped Emma to really figure out what areas she wanted to focus on and how she wanted to represent herself.

So, don't overload your prospective clients with too many services. Business cards aren't just about giving someone your contact details; they should say something about you, through a design or logo, and the particular services you provide.

The same lesson can be applied to postcards and flyers. The simpler the design and message the more professional you will come across. Attaching a postcard, flyer, or business card to a CV and posting it in can be a nice touch and is a good way of attracting the eye of your intended client, who will probably have a mountain of CVs to sift through on any given day. Again, these materials aren't expensive to produce and are well worth investing in as a way of promoting you and your business.

Alarm Bell

Think carefully about how big a print run you order for things like business cards and postcards. Charlie has an enormous box in her loft full of promotional bookmarks she had printed and can now do nothing with because the phone number on them is out of date!

SENDING MAILSHOTS

'Mailshots' is marketing speak for writing to people soliciting work. Charlie in particular found this a very useful way to bring in work in the early days of her business. After all, publishing is a business based on writing, so publishing contacts can respond well to a written approach.

Here are the two things you should include in your mailshot:

☐ **Letter:** Make it concise, professional, and friendly. And, above all, tailor each to the publishing house – for example, explaining why you'd really like to proofread crime thrillers or why you have the experience to design coffee-table book covers. No publisher will be impressed with a one-size-fits-all generic letter.

☐ **CV or experience breakdown:** You aren't applying for a job, so don't feel you need to include details like the Saturday job you had when you were 15 or your GCSE Home Economics grade. Keep it relevant – what skills, experience, and qualifications do you have that back up your freelancing?

Always find out the name of the person you want to send your CV to. Addressing your envelope to 'The Editor, Random House, London' is too vague and will, more than likely, mean your letter never reaches the desired person.

Alarm Bell

Although you can send out e-mailshots (mass emailing), we don't recommend it unless a publisher specifically requests on their website that you contact them for freelancing via email. Your emails will probably end up as SPAM, will never get read, or, worse still, will annoy a potential client whose pet peeve is unsolicited emails.

BUILDING YOUR OWN WEBSITE

Marketing a new business can be expensive, but if you shop around there are many cheap and affordable ways to promote your services. One way of saving money is to build your own website. This may sound like the most arduous task ever, but if you know your way around a PC there's no reason why you can't create your own digital business card and save yourself a bit of cash. Of course, if you have the budget, then you can always invest in a web design company to do the job for you, but it will cost you!

During Emma's first year of business, she realized she couldn't afford to hire the services of a web design company (unless she didn't plan to eat for a few months), so she did a bit of digging and ended up buying a suspiciously cheap version of Dreamweaver (a web design software application) off eBay. Many days of fiddling around later, and she had a brand new site up on the web. However, there are easier ways to do a DIY job when it comes to getting your own site up and running.

Many websites offer free templates, with easy-to-follow instructions about how to design and publish your site on the web. The quality really depends on how complicated or flashy you want your site to be. But if you just want a simple few pages that tell the browser who you are and what you do for a living, then use the more budget-conscious method – you can always upgrade your site as you start to make more money.

Get your website up and running as quickly as you can, as the sooner it's on the web, the quicker you'll rise up the search engine rankings.

Naming your site

Think of a catchy domain name (xxxx.co.uk or xxxx.com) that really describes the services you offer. Some people might use the word 'freelance' in the title, while others might simply use their own name. However, until you're well-established, it's probably better to avoid using your name, as it won't tell your target market what you do for a living or the services you provide.

For most freelancers, their domain name is based on their company name. For usability and search engine optimization, ideally your domain will be all one word – like perfectlywrite.co.uk. But some company names don't lend themselves to this style. For example, Therapist Writer becomes *therapistwriter*, Editors Exchange becomes *editorsexchange*, and AF Art becomes *afart*. So think carefully before choosing a catchy, simple domain name.

Once the light bulb has clicked on, then register the domain name immediately with a domain name registrar. There's nothing more annoying than coming up with the perfect website name, only to find it's already been taken by someone else (who isn't doing it as much justice as you would have!). Even if you don't plan on setting up your site straightaway, securing the name means that nobody else will be able to use it.

Researching your competition

Check out competitor websites: see how they do it and think about how you could do it better. Don't be afraid of contacting your competitors to ask for advice. The freelance world is a generous one, and most people are happy to provide you with some information.

Adding content

There are many ways you can design your site, but the key is to keep it simple! Overloading your web pages with thousands of words of text is one way to keep your prospective clientele at bay. Break content into short paragraphs of 50 to 70 words per section, and use subheadings. People tend to read more slowly when reading off a screen, so make sure your content is eye-catching enough to make them stick around.

This may also sound a bit obvious, but make sure you don't have any glaring typos on your website, especially if you're promoting yourself as a copy editor or proofreader! After all, if you can't write your own site without making mistakes, how do you expect anyone else to trust you to do a meticulous job on their manuscript? Emma was mortified when a completely random person contacted her to point out the absence of an apostrophe on one of her web pages. Embarrassing though this can be, it's better to know about a mistake sooner rather than later, then you can correct it straightaway and put those blushes behind you!

When it comes to proofreading your site, you're often too close to the material to notice typos. It's best to get someone else to read it for you. And that's where collaborating with your 'frenemies' (see Chapter 7) comes in handy – you can ask a proofreading freelancer to check your site in return for doing them a favour.

Designing your site

It can be tempting to get a bit carried away with putting lots of images on your site, but remember the old adage: keep it simple! Too many borrowings from stock photography sites can make your site look messy and distracting. However, research has shown that the top left corner of your web page (known as the 'Golden Square') is the best place to insert a logo or an image, as this is where the eye is most drawn to when viewing a website.

 If design isn't your forte, don't waste countless hours tinkering with how your website looks.

Charlie has certainly been guilty of this in the past – spending days at a time trying to fathom software like Photoshop, Illustrator, and Dreamweaver. But often, your time is best spent doing your client work and getting someone else to do the design work. For example, one of Charlie's best friends, Sarah, is a web designer, and they have a skills swap arrangement – Charlie writes, edits, and proofreads text for Sarah, and Sarah helps Charlie out with design stuff.

Choosing a web host

Once you've designed your website, you need someone to run it for you. There are millions of web host providers out there, and most of them do a good job without charging the earth!

Marketing your site

Once your site is up and running, don't forget about it! Actively updating your site and continually marketing your services can help to secure a loyal client base.

Attract your audience by:

☐ **Adding testimonials to your site:** Once you do a job for a client, ask if you can publish a testimonial from them (saying how great you are!) on your website. Try to get as many of these as possible. Trust is a big thing in the freelance world, and it helps to prove to potential clients that others have been happy with your services.

☐ **Starting a blog:** Blogging is a great way to secure your own audience. Once people see that you're regularly updating your website with an entertaining piece, then they're more likely to come back.

☐ **Linking to other websites:** One of the best ways to get business and improve your rankings is to get other freelancers to add a link to their sites, directing potential clients to your site. You may wonder why on earth your competition would want to give you business, but freelancers specialize in different areas. For example, Emma has an arrangement with another freelancer who directs all writing assignments to her, and she returns the favour with other types of work.

Of course, there are a million more ways you can market your site on the internet and we go into more detail about this in Chapter 6 on digital marketing. However, the first step is to get that website sorted so you can really put yourself on the digital map. Building a website can be a difficult and time-consuming process, but if you get it right, it will really boost your business, and surely that's a worthwhile investment of your time.

SELLING YOURSELF

You can arm yourself with as many pretty postcards and business cards as you want, but none of these will be in any way effective unless you're able to sell yourself to prospective clients. For all the latest technology and digitization, nothing beats good old-fashioned face-to-face contact when you're trying to build a reputation. Most people prefer to do business with someone they've actually met rather than through an anonymous cold call. Sitting down and having a chat with your target client is an invaluable way of gaining their trust and, by getting to know you, the client will be more likely to put some work your way.

Getting on the phone

So, how do you go about actually meeting the people you want to do business with? Let's face it, networking isn't for the faint-hearted: some people love it, while it sends others into a catatonic state of fear. However, sometimes making the effort to meet people on a more personal level is far easier than using the alternative methods of communication.

Emma hates, hates, HATES cold-calling people (phoning people you don't know to try to build a business relationship). She finds it nerve-wracking and totally mortifying. It's true that there can be a sense that you're really bothering someone else, a person who's never met you, never heard of you, and has no idea why you chose them to annoy on that particular day. Think about how irritated you get sometimes when somebody from a call centre rings you up out of the blue and tries to sell you something you don't want or need.

 Before you pick up the phone, prepare exactly what you're going to say. Rehearse out loud if you have to – it really helps!

Of course, cold-calling can reap rewards, and we're not saying you'll necessarily get a bad response from the person at the other end of the phone. One of the best approaches to take when cold-calling is to try and get an introduction to the person you want to speak to. For example, Emma spent months agonizing over whether she should cold-call editors in various publishing houses. She knew that with a little bit of courage she could try and sell herself over the phone, but totally lacked the nerve to do it. When she was at a book fair, she happened to get into a conversation with an in-house copy editor who suggested that Emma mention her name when she called the editor, as an introduction. This makes cold-calling a lot easier, as at least a connection has been established between you and the person you're trying to contact.

 Is there anybody you know who can provide an introduction to the person you want to contact?

Throwing yourself into the fray

It stands to reason that the best way to meet other people in the same business as you is to attend those events that are as specific to your area of the industry as possible.

Not so long ago, business in the publishing world was conducted in what we would call nowadays an 'old school' sort of way. The relationships between editors and their authors would be carried out on a more personal level and manuscripts would be discussed over long, enjoyable lunches at 'The Ivy' and other salubrious eateries. In today's time-sensitive and pressured world, we would gasp at the sheer waste of time and money invested in this seemingly frivolous behaviour. However, despite how it might look nowadays, there was real value in some of the aspects of how business was conducted: the value of building long-lasting relationships.

So, if you have a cold-calling phobia like Emma, or worry that your emails and letters aren't generating the response you want, then the best and easily most effective way of selling yourself and your services and attracting business is by simply talking to others in person. Networking is absolutely key to your new business. Some people fear networking and associate it with the horror of public speaking but, if you get enough practice, it will soon become second nature.

Here's how you can get started:

- ☐ Make a list of all the upcoming events relevant to your business.
- ☐ Make a list of target clients you'd like to chat to at the event.
- ☐ Dress professionally (smart casual) and don't forget your business cards!
- ☐ Don't let yourself leave the event (no matter how awkward you feel) until you've made some form of contact with at least ten people on your list.

When Emma first started out as a freelancer, she had to force herself to attend industry events. She was new to the publishing world, had no real experience or client list, and really dreaded approaching people and striking up a conversation. The first event she attended was the London Book Fair, a huge and overwhelming affair chock-full of publishers' stands as far as the eye can see. With no idea where to start, she began to wander around aimlessly, totally intimidated in an environment where everybody seemed to know everybody else.

Sweating with nerves and feeling a bit tearful, Emma decided to sit down for a little while and think about whether she was going to put on a brave face and conquer her nerves or make a run for it. There happened to be a nice man sitting beside her who started to chat to her. It turned out he was a writer of books on the occult and was also trying to get up the nerve to pitch his ideas to publishers. Between the pair of them, they made a deal to each approach different stands and talk to people there, and report back how it had gone.

Emma went and introduced herself to an editor at a small publishing house who ushered her to sit down and chat further, and Emma ended up gaining a client that day. Indeed, the more stands she approached, the more confident she began to feel, and suddenly she found herself out of business cards! As for the writer, she never saw him again, but credits him for giving her the boost she needed to get started on building her client relationships.

So, the golden rules are: always take advantage of every opportunity, no matter what, and always introduce yourself with a smile and a business card!

Emma once found herself in a black cab with four publishing executives on the way to Heathrow Airport. It sounds like the beginning of a joke, but these are the sort of coincidences that actually happen. Emma didn't take long handing out her business cards and pitching her services to the other experts, who had no choice but to sit there and listen! Again, she managed to get some work out of that chance meeting, so never underestimate the opportunities that a seemingly odd situation can present!

Joining publishing groups and societies

Groups and societies are a great way to meet people and a wonderful avenue for picking up tips about the business. As freelance editors, both Charlie and Emma found the Society of Young Publishers (SYP) to be an excellent source of information and a good way of socializing with others in the same field. Set up over 50 years ago, the SYP aims to provide information and advice to those working in publishing, or wanting to break into the industry (and actually these days the name's a misnomer – membership is open to all ages). They are based in London and Oxford, but many members travel from all over the country to attend their excellent events. The membership fee is more than affordable and the quality of speakers they have is second to none.

Guest speakers include experts in the industry who give talks on anything from marketing, publicity, and children's book publishing to commissioning and editorial roles. Even better, after the event the members are encouraged to meet in the pub down the road to mingle with the speakers and ask them more questions. The SYP also provides a newsletter called *InPrint*, which includes articles about publishing and upcoming events. Both Charlie and Emma met through the SYP and both have written columns about freelancing for *InPrint* magazine.

 What kinds of groups and societies are local to your area? Make a list and sign up!

Moreover, if you happen to have written a book that has been published by a known publisher, then you're eligible to join the rather prestigious Society of Authors (SOA). However, the society doesn't just limit itself to authors, but accepts ghostwriters, academics, broadcasters, illustrators, and translators. Boasting Lord Tennyson, Shaw, Barrie, and Wells as some of their former members, the society also protects the rights of authors and provides advice on publishing contracts and the legal side of being an author. It's more expensive to join than the SYP but well worth it, if only for their informative quarterly journal, *The Author*. Again, the SOA organizes events, meetings, and seminars on industry-related topics, and provides a fantastic networking opportunity for freelancers.

Subscribing to other publications is also a really good way to familiarize yourself with the publishing world. A great source of information for freelancers is *The Bookseller* weekly magazine, which offers the most up-to-date information about the publishing world and includes a handy job section at the back.

Of course, there is a whole host of other groups and organizations you can join, not to mention publications to subscribe to. We've provided a list of some recommended ones in the Useful Contacts section at the end of this book.

WORKING FOR FREE

So, you have your website all set up, your business cards safely installed in your wallet, and your flyers/postcards have been printed off ready to be posted to your target clients. You've just signed up to several groups and societies and have booked your ticket for the next book fair. What next? Working for free, of course!

This may not sound like the most appealing of suggestions and it's an area of the freelance world that nobody likes to talk about. 'Why on earth would I want to start my own business only to work for nothing?' I hear you cry. But working for free doesn't mean the end of your business, or your dignity come to think of it – it can have very positive results and lead to a great deal of paid work.

Now, let's distinguish between how publishers view the 'working for free' concept versus the freelance perspective. Some publishers take on students during the summer months. This can be valuable work experience and very helpful in making contacts in the publishing world. However, there are some publishers that 'employ' interns from six months to a year, without paying them a penny (or a very low wage) and with no guarantee of a job at the end of it. This is nothing more than cheap labour, but hundreds of students, or freelancers who want to try their hand working in-house, line up to apply for these internships. This is because the publishing world is so competitive that many think this is their best way to gain experience and secure a role. In fairness, some interns do get a job at the end of it, but many don't and are left broke and jobless by the end of their contracts. This isn't working for free; this is exploitation.

Alarm Bell

If you get an offer to do some non-fee-paying work, ask yourself what's in it for you!

What we mean by working for free is doing some work that helps promote you and the services you're offering. For example, we both write a column called 'Freelance Glance' for the SYP magazine *InPrint*. We don't get paid for it, but the column helps to showcase our individual talents and writing skills, and has attracted a bit of a following, which has resulted in new industry contacts. The magazine only comes out on a quarterly basis so that's four columns of 800 words every year. It doesn't take up that much time and it's a great way to advertise our services.

Working for free means picking and choosing those projects that will enhance your reputation and generate new business.

At the beginning of her career, Emma made a huge mistake by writing a book proposal on behalf of a client who intended to submit it to publishers. She spent months (including working on Christmas Day!) writing and refining the proposal without being paid a penny for it. Of course, when the publishers rejected the idea for the book, she realized she'd worked for free for all those months with nothing to show for it.

There are two lessons to be learned here:

☐ Don't put all your eggs in one basket.
☐ Always make some financial agreement with your client before you start a piece of work! See Chapter 4 for more advice about rates.

Hindsight is a wonderful thing and Emma learned a tough lesson: never work for free unless you're guaranteed a good result.

SUMMARY

Before you start trading, invest some time and effort into marketing yourself and your business:

✓ Establish a defined marketing strategy and include a budget.

✓ Create business cards and other materials if you want to, but keep them clear and simple!

✓ Send out letters rather than emails, and keep the contents relevant and professional.

✓ Build your own website or, if you have the money, hire a web design company to do it for you.

✓ Sign up for industry events and go out and meet people. Networking is key to business success!

✓ Join groups and societies relevant to your business area.

✓ Work for free, but only if it enhances your reputation and generates new business.

6

KEEPING UP WITH THE KIDS: DIGITAL MARKETING

The internet is one of the greatest opportunities freelancers have ever had to promote themselves in a global market. The strength of advertising over the internet can't be underestimated and, for the budget-conscious freelancer (that is, all of us), there's no cheaper way to market your business. But free marketing comes at a price and often at the expense of your reputation. If you don't know how to effectively increase your online presence, you could end up creating a rather poor impression within one of the biggest media in the world.

Given that it's such a hot topic these days, it's surprising how little we know about digital marketing and how it all works. Essentially, digital marketing means promoting your services through various channels such as the internet, mobile phones, and instant messaging (IM). For the purposes of this chapter, we've chosen to focus on marketing your business online and how to build a significant online presence.

When we were setting up our businesses, we knew how important it was to have a website, but had no idea how to optimize it or use it to attract new business. Therefore, our sites never made into the rankings and we never got much business from them. However, once we started to look into it, we realized there were dozens of things we could do to promote our services online, and got stuck in!

So, before you launch headlong into the virtual world, make sure you do your research and figure out your own online strategy.

GETTING RANKED

One of the most important ways for your website to attract business is to have it listed on the first page of search engine results, making sure your site is as high in the rankings as possible. Think about it: if you're searching for something on the web, do you ever make it past page one? Most people rarely scroll to the bottom of the first page, let alone click to the next one. We're a fickle and impatient lot when it comes to browsing the web, and don't have time to be going through pages and pages of content. So, it stands to reason that page one is exactly where you need to be.

This is where search engine optimization (SEO) comes in. SEO is a method whereby you create and improve a website so that it will rank high in the search engines. You may have a vague idea about SEO and how it all works, but the truth is that it's such a vast subject that we could write several volumes on it and still have more to say.

SEO techniques also change on a regular basis, so it's wise to keep up with the ever-fluctuating ways to enhance your website so you're not left behind. To ensure that we've provided you with the most up-to-date website-enhancing information, we've asked one of the experts, Miles Galliford, to give you some tips about how you can increase your digital presence while keeping your valuable reputation intact (see the later section 'Over to the experts', p.112).

Weaving in keywords

Keywords are big news for SEO. They're basically the words you want someone to search for you with and find you in a search engine. For example, some of our keywords are ghostwriter, copy-editor, proofreader, book critique, author mentoring (you'll notice some are more key terms than keywords as they comprise more than one word).

You need to *subtly* weave your target keywords into:

☐ the text on your website

☐ the source code (the code that drives your site) – in the tags for page title, page description (the text that comes up in a search engine's results for a page) and keywords.

 Alarm Bell

Don't make the mistake of thinking you must cram your key-words into your site wherever possible, to the detriment of sense and good writing.

First of all, the clever people who run search engines are wise to this ploy, and it doesn't necessarily follow that keywords all over the shop equals a high ranking. For example, we know freelancers who list all their keywords at the bottom of every web page (sometimes in 'invisible' text that no one can read except the search engine spiders), and this is frowned upon as being poor and unfair SEO practice. Plus, if you take keyword-stuffing to the extreme, you're left with text that sounds ridiculous and puts the reader off with its crass and obvious attempt at SEO, like this:

> *Welcome to the Book Marketing Guru, a site dedicated to book marketing and run by a book marketing expert whose experience in book marketing and skills in book marketing are second to none. Book marketing is all about marketing books, and as a book marketing professional I have a wealth of knowledge in the field of book marketing.*

Gah! Who'd want to hire this person, even if they are number one in the rankings?

Linking is the key

Linking to other websites and getting others to link to your website is one of the most powerful ways to achieve high rankings. Google, BBC, YouTube, and Facebook are among the most popular sites in the UK. So, if you link your entry on Facebook to your site and vice versa, you'll be well on your way to achieving high-ranking status! Better still – imagine if you found a way to publish something on the BBC website. The article would include a link to your website from one of the most traffic-heavy websites in the UK. The BBC is great for hanging on to archives, so the link to your website could be there for years, boosting your rankings every day!

 How can you create your own linking network to boost your rankings?

SOCIALIZING VIRTUAL-STYLE

Social networking has become the new way of mingling and making contacts. Barack Obama managed to secure one of the most powerful positions in the world with the help of social networking sites, so there's no reason why you can't use them to your advantage.

Setting up a presence on these sites (Facebook, MySpace, Twitter, and so on) is easy and best of all, free! LinkedIn is particularly useful as it links to other people in similar professions within a network of trusted contacts. The more connections you make through the 'friend of a friend' method, the less likely it is that you receive bogus or random enquiries. LinkedIn is one of Emma's favourite social networking tools as it has attracted more work than any of the others, so far.

Emma was asked to write a business book by a major publisher purely because she had invited the editor (with whom she'd worked on a previous project a couple of years before) to join LinkedIn. Coincidentally, the editor was on the look-out for an author with business experience to write a book about a top entrepreneur, and the invitation Emma sent served to jog her memory, prompting her to ask Emma if she was available to take on that particular project.

We know that social networking can be a useful forum for broadcasting your services and making new contacts, but not all of them are the same, so which ones should you choose? Here are some facts from Ofcom, the communications regulator in the UK, about the most popular social networking sites:

□ The most popular social networking sites are MySpace, Facebook, and Bebo.

□ On average, most adult social networkers have a profile on more than one social networking site, which they check frequently.

□ Facebook is the most popular site for adults with 62 per cent having an online profile.

□ Bebo has captured 62 per cent of the total children and young adults' market.

So, before signing up to all social networking sites in existence, think about the services you're promoting and the market you'd like to target. After all, it's not much use building a profile on Bebo if you're trying to attract a predominantly adult market.

If you're using Twitter, use it to promote yourself and your specialist area, not to complain about your personal woes!

GOING VIRAL

Viral marketing means word-of-mouth, digital style. Theoretically, you might publish some original content on your website and your social networking sites or create a video that demonstrates the message you're trying to promote. If your audience likes it, then they'll pass it on to their friends, who will – hopefully – like it enough to share with their friends, and so on. Suddenly, your content ends up being read by thousands more people than you could ever have imagined! You find yourself inundated with new queries and clients pestering to invest in your services. Sounds simple, doesn't it?

However, viral marketing is pretty tricky. It can be hard to predict what will appeal to your target market and what will fall flat. Sometimes, viral marketing campaigns are just about pure luck. It also helps if you already have a solid following that's been cultivated over time. A trusted network of contacts goes a long way in helping you to spread the word over the net. So, if you feel you have something unique to promote, then it's worth getting a bit creative and thinking up ideas about how to make your service stand out from the crowd.

The author Lorelei Mathias launched a successful viral marketing campaign to promote her debut novel, *Step On It, Cupid*. You can read her inspirational story in Chapter 10, p.206.

PAYING FOR THE PRIVILEGE

So far we've spoken about free marketing on the internet, but what about paid advertising? There are many ways you can advertise online without paying too much, and this can help to give you the exposure you need. For example, there are some freelancing job sites out there that allow you to add your profile to their website for a fee. This gives you another medium to advertise your services, while adding yet another link to your own website. If you're going to go down this route, then make sure that the freelancing site ranks very highly in the search engine listings – the higher the ranking, the more lucrative it will be for your personal business site.

Alarm Bell

Only pay for advertising if you've done your research and are absolutely sure that you will get your money's worth.

Ever wonder how people manage to get their ads published on the right side of the screen on the Google listings page? Google AdWords allows you to create an ad tailored to the most relevant keywords to your business. For example, if you're a freelance copy editor, you would use 'copy editor' in your ad, and any time that keyword was entered by someone else in the Google search engine, your ad would pop up on the right-hand side of the screen next to the search results – which is more eye-catching than being lost in the hundreds of pages of results. Google AdWords works on a cost-per-click basis and allows you to set your own budget as to how much you want to spend every time someone clicks on your ad.

Google also has a free tool called Google Keyword, which tells you the monthly search volume for your chosen keyword. Of course, the more popular the keyword, the more successful your ad will be. So, if 'copy editor' generates 5,000 more searches every month than just 'book editor', for example, then it's best to use the most favoured keyword.

To be honest, we've never paid to advertise through cost-per-click on the web, so we're not setting ourselves up as experts in the field. The reason for this is that both of us work off slightly different business models: although Emma has a website, she depends primarily on word-of-mouth for generating new business, while Charlie receives the majority of her custom through her SEO website. So far we haven't found it necessary to pay to advertise online, but we've certainly not ruled it out! Freelancing is an uncertain business, and if it looks like we're facing a drought, we might well consider investing in paid online advertising.

There are lots of different ways to advertise on the internet, and pay for the privilege, but we don't have room for all of them here. So if you have the time and the budget, get online and research other advertising methods that might help attract more browsers to your business. Off the top our heads, we'd suggest you might find the following useful if you're looking to place an ad:

☐ Google AdSense
☐ Google AdWords
☐ Yahoo! Search Marketing
☐ Microsoft adCenter.

MAINTAINING YOUR DIGITAL PRESENCE

Staying ahead of the competition and attracting prospective clients means constantly maintaining your visibility on the web. Working on something new? Update your profile on LinkedIn or Facebook and make sure your contacts know the type of work you're involved in. If your contacts happen to come across someone who needs a hand with a project that's along the same lines as the one you've just broadcast, then they're likely to recommend you.

It's no good just signing up to these social networking sites and imagining the work will flow in. As with your website, you need to keep updating the information on these sites to ensure your online presence is still active. The more maintenance you do, the better the result(s).

BLOGGING FOR YOUR SUPPER

Blogging is a great way to showcase your own work and your personality on the internet. Sites such as blogging.com and wordpress.com allow you to publish your blogs for free. So, *why* would you blog on these sites when you have a perfectly good website of your own to blog away on? Well, again, the trick is all about linking. The chances are these blogging websites rank well above yours in the search engine listings; therefore, if you link your blog on blogging.com to your own personal site, and vice versa, then this will help move you up the rankings.

These days, a lot of communication takes place electronically, which although convenient and time-saving doesn't make up for personal contact. Your website is the only medium you have to show that you're a trustworthy, reliable, committed, and all-round genuinely nice person – and you must convey that message to visitors to your site, before they even contact you!

In a real-life job interview, you can (perhaps!) afford to make a lukewarm first impression as long as you make up for it during the time allowed (and if you have a nice interviewer!). One false statement or off-colour comment on your website and you'll lose potential clients you never even knew you had. This is where blogging comes in.

Writing about your field in an interesting, friendly, relatable, and original way sets you up as an expert, and portrays you as someone who really knows their stuff. People who are going to invest time and money into hiring you will want to know that you're trustworthy and safe to deal with. Your blog can help determine whether people take that next step and contact you or skip on to another website.

Keep your blog up to date, informative, friendly, engaging, and to the point!

Blogging is a discipline in itself. Writing a blog requires time and dedication. It's not enough to write a blog one day and leave a two-month gap before your next blog entry. If you do, the legion of followers you'd attracted to your site will have deserted you at this stage, and you'd end up staunching the departing flow of much-needed traffic. Being a bit cavalier when it comes to blog updates is something we're both guilty of, especially when we're really busy. However, it's important to be disciplined when maintaining your site; all it takes is a few minutes out of your day, and it's a worthwhile investment of your time.

SEEING IS BELIEVING

We mention working for free in Chapter 5 and the benefits it can bring if approached in the right way. Publishing free content online on a regular basis is a great way of attracting a loyal following, and will help generate new business. Free content can be anything from providing top tips in your specialist field to publishing an article with a website such as ezinearticles.com.

For example, Charlie's website contains articles on freelancing and writing tips. From checking Google Analytics each month, Charlie can see that quite a few visitors to her site come through these articles – they type something like 'affect or effect' into Google and come through to her article called 'Words to watch'. Some visitors then click around the site; others read that article and then leave. These may not be potential clients, but each time your website ranks for a search term in a search engine and a user clicks through, you're improving your SEO.

The difficulty that most people have when it comes to digital marketing is the amount of time it takes to learn and apply this ever increasing scale of knowledge to their own business. Yes, it can be time-consuming, and definitely challenging when it comes to balancing so many plates (or sites) in the air, but once you see the results of your efforts, you'll be glad that you invested some time in promoting yourself online.

OVER TO THE EXPERTS: THE FREELANCER'S GUIDE TO BUILDING YOUR REPUTATION ON THE INTERNET

Miles Galliford is the Co-founder/Director of SubHub.com. SubHub are experts at making money from content on the internet. They help individuals, publishers, and organizations to launch their websites, publish content online, and generate multiple revenue streams.

'Today, you are who the web says you are. It's critical for everyone to understand this lesson, particularly graduates, freelancers, small business owners, and individuals whose value is based on their knowledge and expertise. Therefore, it is critical that you do as much as you can to control your reputation on the internet.

Building a really strong reputation is about becoming known for being an expert in one niche subject. When writing for the web your goal is to let both your expertise and your personality shine through.

The benefits of managing your online reputation are as follows.

☐ The web is your most powerful tool for getting a great job or new contracts.

☐ It is a very cost-effective way of promoting yourself.

☐ You can reach a global audience.

☐ You can build your authority and credibility way beyond just qualifications.

☐ You can use networks and communities to attract work or new roles.

☐ You can find new business partners and opportunities.

☐ It's fun.

The disadvantages of online promotion are as follows.

☐ It can be very time-consuming.

☐ It can be challenging to keep up with changes.

☐ You can't unpublish anything that goes on the web.

How much control can you have?

You can't control what others write about you on the internet and, worse still, once something is on the web it's there forever. However, if you are publishing stuff regularly, then this is the stuff that should find its way to the top of the search results when people search for your name. This is what searchers will base their first impressions on.

The HEART rule of great content

When writing for the web always remember the HEART rule. Make sure everything you publish is:

☐ Honest

☐ Exclusive

☐ Accurate

☐ Relevant

☐ Timely

Top tips for your website

Your home should always be your own personal website, although it's fine to have a presence on other third-party sites such as Facebook and MySpace.

Use your website to build your credibility and authority in your area of expertise. Quote and link to other experts to show your connection to the field.

Your domain name is one of your most important assets. Don't let anyone else be in control of it.

Going multimedia

The future of the web is multimedia. Photos, video, and audio are becoming universal on large and small websites alike. It's time for you to jump on this bandwagon. Buy a cheap camcorder (for example, the Flip Mino) and start getting used to doing short video clips. Post them on YouTube and embed them on your site. Publish interesting photos to Flickr and possibly interviews on iTunes. Multimedia can be fun, valuable and make you stand out from the pack.

Alerting and tracking

An important part of managing your online reputation is always being aware of what people are saying about you and the subject you are interested in. There are some simple free tools that can help you stay on top. Set up a Google Alert for your name and any other phrases you are interested in tracking. Create a Google Reader account to track new posts from the blogs you follow. Set up Tweetdeck on your PC and add a 'Mentions' column to track your name in the Twittersphere.

Getting loved by the search engines

Understanding how the search engines work is critical to understanding how you can take greater control over your online reputation. You need to ensure the important information about you shows up on the first page of the search results when people do a search on your name. If you don't state the content you control on page one, it means someone else is in control of your online reputation; not a good situation to be in!

Google promotes pages up the search results ranking by looking at a few important criteria:

- ☐ They match the words the searcher is looking for, such as your name, with the words on a site. There should be an exact match.

- ☐ They look for a repetition of these words in the title, headings, and body text.

- ☐ They look for how many other websites link to that page. These inbound links act as testimonials or endorsements for the site. The more links, the more valuable Google perceives that content to be, and the higher it ranks the page.

Therefore, to ensure your website gets a high ranking, you must put your name on every page and also think about how people will search for you. If you have a common name, searchers will probably add additional keywords to identify you, such as your company name, your area of expertise, your university, your location, and so on. Make sure you mention all of these additional keywords on your site so they are connected to your name.

Bringing all your online activity together

Everything you publish on the web is part of your reputation and online personality. Think carefully about what you say and how you say it. Everything anyone else publishes about you is also part of your reputation. You can't tell people what to write, but helping others without expectation of anything in return can influence what people say.

I recommend that you split your time 50:50 between publishing to your own site and contributing to third-party sites (including the social networks). Quality is more important than quantity, but publishing regularly will keep you in the spotlight.

Make sure whenever possible you link back to your site from any and all third-party sites. Don't be afraid to ask for links. Google has to love your site or you will remain out of site, out of mind.

Remember, you are who the web says you are. '

CASE STUDY: CREATIVE MARKETING

Andrew Crofts is an author and ghostwriter. He has published around 80 books, a dozen of which have been *Sunday Times* number one bestsellers, and some of which have enjoyed equal success around the world. (*Sold*, which he wrote for Zana Muhsen, has now sold around four million copies in various international editions.) He is the author of *The Freelance Writer's Handbook* and *Ghostwriting* (which Robert Harris quoted from extensively in his recent bestseller *The Ghost*, now a film by Roman Polanski). In 2008 he published a novel, *The Overnight*

Fame of Steffi McBride, which is about the cost of instant fame, and he is following it up with *The Fabulous Dreams of Maggie de Beer*.

❛Marketing has always been a problem for writers, firstly because there are so many people fighting for the attention of readers and secondly because reading anything is time-intensive, which makes it hard to reach potential clients quickly and effectively. If you are a singer you only have to hold people's attention for the two or three minutes of a song, an artist only needs a few seconds to make a visual impact with a painting, but a novelist probably needs at least six or seven hours of their audience's time.

When I started out as a freelance writer at the age of 16 in 1970 I had two ways of marketing myself; one was to send out work on spec in the hope that someone would buy it, the second was to beg for commissions and opportunities to show them what I could do.

My target market consisted of book publishers, book agents (to a much lesser extent than today), newspaper and magazine editors and anyone else who might hire the services of writers, like public relations people. The only medium to reach them at all cost effectively was the post. As a result I would send out hundreds of letters a week, knowing that even a one per cent response rate would be enough to keep me going.

I would print up leaflets promoting myself as a "business writer" or a "travel writer", or whatever brand I thought would appeal to my next target market, constantly hunting out new lists of names and addresses.

By 1990 I had discovered the potential goldmine of ghostwriting and that gave me a unique selling point and a brand that I could promote more effectively. I started taking advertisements in *The*

Bookseller and *Publishing News*, headed "Ghostwriter for Hire". I wanted to ensure that my name and telephone number were constantly available to anyone who might be looking for ghostwriting services – a bit like putting up a card in the post office window of the "publishing village". The response rate was low, maybe two or three books a year, but the projects that did come through were profitable enough to be able to keep the campaign running for 20 years.

Then came the internet and the possibility to set up a permanent shop window for my goods and services in the form of a website – www.andrewcrofts.com. All I had to do then was to find ways to direct people to the site or to make it more likely that they would find their own way there.

Through my general ghostwriting site I now receive about four approaches a day from prospective clients – more than enough to choose from. The marketing challenge is then finding ways to help to sell those projects to agents, publishers, and the general public. The website, however, has raised my profile in those areas too, which helps with the selling process. People are always more willing to put in the time to read a submission from someone they have heard of.

When I published a novel in 2008 called *The Overnight Fame of Steffi McBride*, I decided to use similar marketing methods. I created a separate website for the book itself, which was linked to Amazon for anyone who was tempted to buy, and then created content to make the website interesting in itself.

One of my daughters is an actress, so I made her the face of Steffi and made a video with her talking as the character, which went up onto YouTube and played constantly on the website. I ran a competition for other people wanting to write books about "instant fame", offering mentoring services for the winner. Both these initiatives gave journalists something to write about. I dipped my toe into the Twittering and Facebook pools, with limited success. Probably books need to grow organically out of those media rather than the other way around.

Overall the efforts did not make *Steffi* a huge bestseller, but they created enough interest for the publisher to commission a follow-up (actually a prequel, starring Steffi's mother, a wannabe star and occasional vice girl from the Seventies and Eighties, which is titled *The Fabulous Dreams of Maggie de Beer*), and I had another daughter who could become 'the face' of the character on the cover of that book – extending the brand and the publishing story.

The marketing difficulties facing writers in 2010 are really no different to the ones of 1970. If anything, the levels of competitive noise have risen in the last 40 years as more people have gained access to keyboards, and the amount of time people have available for reading has become even less. The internet, however, has provided every writer with the opportunity to create their own shop window and public relations platform at a very low cost. It has put power into all our hands, so the trick now is learning the skills necessary to use that power to achieve a genuine marketing advantage or sales results. '

SUMMARY

If you want to be a digital star, here's how to go about it:

✓ Drive traffic through your website online and offline: online, through optimization; and offline, by encouraging anyone you meet to check it out!

✓ Play with your website and constantly make sure it is up to date and the best it can be.

✓ Link to as many high-ranking sites as you can: social networking sites, your competitors' sites (and get them to link to yours), and any other sites relevant to the services you are offering.

✓ Blog, blog, and blog some more! Blogging is one of the best ways to secure a following and generate business.

✓ Don't think of your website as simply an 'online presence' – think of it as a stepping stone to get you to the best position for attracting new business.

✓ Pay for advertising if you think it will benefit your business, but make sure you do your research before you commit.

✓ Word of mouth is still the best way to attract business, so make sure your digital presence gets tongues wagging!

✓ Be creative! Do your research and launch your own viral marketing campaign.

✓ Not all social networking sites are the same, so do your research and ensure that each one performs a function that serves the right purpose for your business.

✓ Publish articles, extracts, or anything else you can do to showcase your talents, not just on your website but on all the social networking sites that you're registered with.

✓ Grab some books, research on the internet, go to a seminar, or sign up to some classes – whatever method you choose, make sure you know as much as you can about internet marketing before you dive into the virtual world.

7

WORKING WITH FRENEMIES

Most people think that working-from-home freelancing is a solitary affair. You get up, stay in your pyjamas all day, watch some telly, and do some work in between snacking and, well, watching more telly. It's true that some freelancers operate in this way, but not the successful ones! Every freelancer who works from home needs the help and support from others in the business. It can be a lonely experience if you don't have anyone you can talk to who understands the trials and tribulations of your job. Imagine if you were stuck at home every day, without any contact with the outside world, just existing so you could get that proofreading job back to the client on time. That's not much fun, is it?

One of the most valuable ways to connect with the world outside your door and to generate more work (and more income) is to establish a relationship with other freelancers or 'frenemies': your competition. A 'fremeny' is generally someone you're friends with but also regard as an enemy or a competitor. However, in the freelance world, your frenemies are one of the most important assets of your business.

Connecting with others and sharing your experiences is a great way to learn more about the industry and how things are done. Some freelancers are terrified of getting in touch with others working in a similar field for fear that their 'rivals' will somehow undercut them, or poach work from them. However, nothing could be further from the truth.

COLLABORATING WITH YOUR COMPETITORS

Competing against someone else implies that whoever does the quickest, fastest job will receive the reward. In the sports world it stands to reason that those who train the hardest and study the competition will win the gold medal. However, if you're part of a relay team, for example, collaboration is key in order to reach the same goals. In the retail business, competition is healthy, but only if the competitors are striving for the same outcome: producing a quality product that achieves client satisfaction. Indeed, if all the competitors came together to swap and share ideas, there's no doubt that the quality would increase even further, leading to more sales, and more satisfied clients.

The same theory applies to the freelance world. Freelancers operating in isolation miss the chance to learn from others in a similar field, and improve their own skills. It might sound strange to collaborate with your competitors, but this is only if you view your fellow freelancers as rivals or 'the enemy'. Sharing ideas is a great opportunity to pick up some tips and apply them to your own business for the good of the client; the more freelancers producing quality work, the better the freelance reputation, which all leads to an increase in income.

For example, say you offer a book critiquing service as part of your skillset. This job involves reading manuscripts and providing comments on how the author could improve the story, pointing out inconsistencies and repetition, reviewing the structure, and analysing the technical aspects of the manuscript such as writing style, grammar, and spelling. There are no set guidelines for book critiquing so there's always a little room for doubt that you're doing a good job and meeting the right specifications. Then, imagine that you and a fellow freelancer decide to swap notes, and agree to read each other's book critiques, with a view to sharing ideas. The only thing that will stop you from doing this is fear: fear that your colleague will hate your personal style and approach; or fear that your 'rival's' book critique will be much, much better than yours!

However difficult you might find handing over your precious notes to someone else, swapping work is a learning experience; you get to see what mistakes you're making as does the other person. Pride-swallowing is difficult, especially if you think that you're the ultimate expert in book critiques (and you realize you still have a lot to learn). However, if you can do a mindshift and look at collaboration as an opportunity, rather than a threat, then the quality of work and your performance will improve, and that can only mean one thing: more income from more satisfied clients.

 See collaboration as an opportunity, not a threat.

But before you decide to share your experiences with other freelancers, make sure that you make the right connections first. The freelance world is based on trust and you need to find the right people to swap advice with.

RESEARCHING YOUR COMPETITION

Researching your competition is the best way to find out which freelancers you'd like to get in touch with. You'll probably be familiar with some of the main players from the days of building your own website. However, if you're unsure about who would be the most suitable contacts to make, here are some tips:

☐ Get online and do some relevant keyword searches in a search engine such as Google. For example, if you're a freelance copywriter, type this in and see what websites come up.

☐ Carry out more keyword searches in other online communities, such as Facebook, MySpace and LinkedIn, and see how many freelancers have a significant presence online.

☐ Check out advertisements freelancers have placed in trade publications and contact them that way.

☐ Set up Google Alert (as mentioned in Chapter 6) to send you notifications about the subject you're interested in.

☐ Read the magazines published by whatever societies you have joined, and contact freelancers who've written articles for those publications.

☐ Check whether your fellow freelancers have a blog and read it as often as you can to get familiar with their personalities and their working style.

☐ Once you've created a shortlist, email or phone your fellow freelancers and arrange to meet for a coffee, if possible. You'll soon know if you want to add them to your network.

The more you know about your competition before contacting them the better, as this knowledge will help you establish what you have in common, and help build a fruitful and mutually beneficial relationship.

ESTABLISHING CONTACT

There are many ways of introducing yourself to your supposed rivals. Of course, the most effective way is in person, through industry events, for example. But the likelihood of being able to attend all these events is slim, so the next best thing is to send a friendly email, introducing yourself and explaining what you do.

When Emma first started life as a freelancer, she took every opportunity to meet people and introduce herself to all and sundry. However, one of the most valuable contacts she made was the co-author of this book, Charlie Wilson. At the time, Charlie wrote a column about freelancing for a publishing magazine, which Emma read religiously. Emma was similarly impressed with Charlie's website, which contained really useful information and tips about many aspects of freelancing.

One day, Emma decided to drop Charlie a quick email to make contact, but didn't really expect to get any sort of response. To her surprise, Charlie responded straightaway (Emma has since learned that Charlie is the model of efficiency!). A flurry of emails followed, resulting in a meeting which ended with Emma agreeing to take over Charlie's business for the duration of her maternity leave!

This is just one example of how a simple introduction can lead to more work and more income.

PASSING THE BUCK

You may be surprised to hear that most freelancers are relieved when other freelancers get in touch, looking to collaborate on projects or offering their services. As one copywriter put it, 'There's nothing worse than telling a client you're too busy to take on a piece of work, without at least softening the blow by providing them with another contact.' This is true in most areas of our daily lives. If you go into a shop looking for a specific hard-to-find item, don't you appreciate it more when the salesperson tells you that although the store doesn't stock it, they can direct you to a place that does? By advising you to try elsewhere, the salesperson is being helpful and providing good client care, rather than sending you off to the competition. Furthermore, you'll be more likely to go back to that shop because you'll have good memories of how you were treated.

 If you can't take on the work yourself, always offer to refer your client to another expert in the field.

Turning people away is one of the toughest parts of being a freelancer. It's truly the curse of the self-employed that it can either be a feast or famine situation, and sometimes the feast can be far too filling! In those cases, you need to be able to turn people away in such a way that they'll still come back to you with another project down the line.

One of the best ways to do this is to be as helpful and honest as possible. Your reputation is your most valuable asset and it's important that you don't lose out just because you're unable to accept a piece of work. Express interest in their project but explain that you have several others that you're working on and fear you might not have the time to commit fully to their piece of work. This is also a good way of handling it, as it shows that you're busy and in demand, something that appeals to prospective clients. They're also more likely to come back to you in the future.

However, you can suggest that the client contacts a colleague of yours who also has the same experience and would be happy to hear from them. Rather than leaving the client high and dry, this is a more professional way of dealing with the matter. Certainly, it's far better than accepting the piece of work, in spite of your massive workload, and consequently making a shambles of it.

Recommending a fellow freelancer in this situation isn't about 'giving away' valuable work to 'the enemy' who'll then steal all your clients, but a way of helping out your client while building and maintaining a relationship with your fellow freelancer. It also means that the freelancer is sure to return the favour when they encounter a similar situation.

BRANCHING OUT

Over time, you'll find that you have built up a sizeable network of freelancers from various disciplines. But just because you're a full-time copy editor and proofreader doesn't mean that you should only get in touch with others in this area. Getting to know what other freelancers do and how they fit into the publishing model is very important when it comes to learning the business. Staying in your own little bubble stunts knowledge and growth; besides, there might come a time where you may want to progress into other areas of publishing, and it's useful to have an expert on your books that you can contact to discuss your next career move.

FINDING A MENTOR

Irrespective of what sort of business you're in, finding yourself a mentor can be extremely useful. Mentors are usually people who have been in the business longer than you, have far more experience, and are willing to guide you and share some of their own business secrets. Mentors want you to do well and are happy to share the benefits of their experience with you. They don't cost anything, and who in their right mind would turn away free advice?

 Once you find your mentor, never ever let him (or her) go!

Emma found her mentor almost by accident. She was researching books on freelancing and came across one by a well-known author. In fact, she found the book so useful that she researched the author online, looked up his website, and contacted him through the email address he had provided. Emma started off her introductory email by complimenting him on his book, and offering to help him should he ever need a hand with anything. Again, Emma didn't expect to receive a reply from someone so big and important, but sure enough, her soon-to-be mentor replied, thanking her for getting in touch, and expressed relief that he now had another contact in the same business that he could recommend to clients when his workload became unmanageable.

Sure enough, Emma's mentor, who is highly influential in the publishing world, started to suggest her name to clients in his vast network, and Emma started getting lots of enquiries as a result. To this day, most of Emma's work comes through her mentor, who almost acts as her own personal recruitment consultant, without taking a cut of her earnings! However, in order to make an effort to repay her mentor's generosity, Emma does make a point of treating him to lunch once a year!

A mentor is also great when you're struggling with a piece of work, or wondering what on earth you're going to charge a client. A typical conversation between Emma and her mentor with regards to a ghostwriting business project is as follows:

Emma: Thank you for passing on that piece of work to me. I just need your advice about a couple of things.

Mentor: No problem; fire away.

Emma: Well, firstly, the client wants me to write a 200,000 word book on the Bulgarian economy in three months for £10,000, and I don't think that's realistic.

Mentor: Absolutely not. Tell him that a book that length on that subject is going to be tedious and boring for you and the reader. Also, that price he has quoted is unacceptable for a book that length. Renegotiate and let me know how he responds.

Emma: But if I negotiate, I might put him off, and I really want to do this book.

Mentor: Well, think about how many weeks this is going to take you and calculate the daily rate you will be making from writing the project. Think also about the amount of research involved. This isn't a straightforward book, and you need to charge accordingly.

Emma: Okay, I'll give it a try! Thanks so much for the advice. I owe you as per usual!

Mentor: Not at all. Let me know how you get on.

Some people have a commission arrangement set up between themselves and their mentors or fellow freelancers. This means that should one pass work on to the other, the person doing the work will give a commission to the person who's referred them to the client, and vice versa. There's nothing wrong with this, and in some cases it might make sense financially, but in most cases there are no fees exchanged when it comes to passing on work. The freelance community is a generous one and it generally operates on goodwill, which always pays off in the end.

MOTIVATING EACH OTHER

Collaborating with the competition is also a great motivator. As a freelancer, there are days that you lack the self-discipline to get stuck into work. Suddenly, sleeping late or going shopping can seem like far more attractive prospects than wading through hundreds of pages of proofs. Generally, the self-employed depend on two emotions to motivate them: guilt, that every second you spend not working is impacting on your finances; and fear, that you won't get enough work in to pay the rent or mortgage.

 It's better to take some time out than doing a half-hearted job.

However, even these emotions can be swept aside, especially at the end of the week where it can be tempting to go down the 'Freelance Fridays' route. Freelance Fridays mean taking a guilty day off, and treating yourself to a nice lunch or some new clothes when you know deep down that you really don't deserve it. But if you knew that your freelancer pals were all slaving away and generating more business while you were fast asleep, then you would be more motivated to get up and do some work. For example, whenever Emma gets that 'can't be bothered' feeling, she calls up Charlie, who's either in the middle of a whirlwind of activity, or is in the same unmotivated state. Both scenarios are mutually beneficial here:

☐ If Emma is aware that Charlie is drumming up new business and coming up with all sorts of inspirational ideas, Emma will get similarly inspired and start suggesting her own ideas, which will get her back into working mode.

☐ If both Emma and Charlie are able to moan about how much they can't be bothered, they'll feel less guilty about taking time off, but will make a pact to start afresh the next day. Surprisingly, this usually snaps them both out of their paralysed state!

When it comes to freelancing, everyone's different and will be motivated by different things. However, having a close pal in the business that understands everything you're going through and who offers support when necessary is invaluable. In the freelance world, there's nobody standing over you with a whip, and therefore nobody to motivate you or provide you with much-needed advice. There's nobody else to blame if you make a mistake, and the responsibility this brings, together with various blows to your pride when you do mess up, are only easier to deal with when you have someone else to vent to about them.

RANTING ABOUT RATES

One of the most difficult parts of being a freelancer is not knowing how much to charge for a piece of work. Projects come in all shapes and sizes and what you may charge very much depends on the type of work you get in. Although some professional societies suggest rates for services such as editing and proofreading, there's no set rule for other types of projects. Although it sounds like a great thing to be able to charge clients whatever you want, you still a need to find a fair balance between charging too high and charging too low.

So, once again, here's another advantage of getting to know your competition. You can find out how much they charge and think about whether your rates are in a similar league or totally outrageous. Some people aren't comfortable about asking others how much they charge, viewing it as a breach of etiquette (along the same lines as asking someone how much they paid for their house or how much they earn). However, if you make an effort to build a relationship with your fellow freelancers, then there's no reason why you can't discuss this side of the business; indeed, you'll probably find that the other freelancer is as anxious as you to swap notes on rates.

Summon up the courage to talk rates, no matter how awkward it may seem!

 When Charlie first went freelance, she was very much stumbling about in the dark when it came to rates. Proofreading and copy-editing work wasn't too tricky at that point, as her publishing clients were setting the fees, but copywriting was another ball game entirely. Charlie started out charging £15 per hour, thinking that was a good deal more than she was earning in her part-time temp job. But at a networking event she got chatting with an SEO copywriter with several years' experience, and eventually found the courage to ask for advice on rates. The result? She doubled her rate overnight.

For the stealthy few who want to get information fast, without going to the trouble of building a long-lasting relationship with their competition, there's another, sneakier way to get the information you want.

We've received several enquiries over email from people pretending they need a freelancer to help them out on a project. They tend to ask for very detailed information about how the freelance business works, how rates are decided for different pieces of work, and also might ask about invoicing and tax information. Once this pretender has received the information you've provided them, they disappear, never to be heard from again. Generally, the pretender will apply the advice you've given to their own business and probably copy some information off your website or even contact some of your clients if they're listed.

This is one method you can use if you're researching your competition, but it's underhanded and generally frowned upon in the industry. You may find out what you need, but you'll lose out on being able to ever contact that freelancer again. Worse still, if you happen to bump into them in a social setting, it could be a little awkward!

 Alarm Bell

Trust your instincts and follow up on suspicious enquiries.

Spotting bogus versus genuine clients can be tricky, but if you have your suspicions about the authenticity of an enquiry, especially if it's communicated via email, then Google the person's name or the company (if provided) and see if they are the genuine article. In many cases, the person will have provided a false email address, or they might have actually approached you personally and you end up finding their own freelance website, which will probably be furnished with the information you've just provided, or even contain portions of your own website, which have been stolen!

Say you've had an enquiry email from a Jane Brown who wants to know all about you and your services. If you suspect that she's just fishing for information, then make a decision: either just give it to Jane and let her do whatever she wants with it; or simply ignore her email. Frankly, people who operate in such a stealthy manner will probably not make the most of whatever information you provide anyway, so you might not have to worry about giving too much away. Similarly, if she approaches your clients, using your name as a way in, then if you have a good relationship with your clients they'll be sure to let you know.

 TOP TIP

Share business advice with trusted colleagues who are willing to return the favour.

WORKING TOGETHER

Many businesses succeed because they're open to working with their competitors. The message here is that you don't have to hurt other businesses in order to make your business a success. Emma spent a couple of years working for one financial institution where competition within the teams was fierce. Everyone was terrified of giving too much away in case someone else took the credit for their work, and backstabbing was a way of life to get ahead. However, this style of doing business only caused friction within the team, lowered morale, and created a miserable environment to work in.

The freelance world is the exact opposite of this. People are so generous and willing to give support and advice that sometimes you end up wondering what the catch is. When freelancers start working together to swap business ideas, the business can only improve. For example, at first Emma hadn't a clue about rates or what to charge clients, and ended up charging much lower than she should have (and then wondered why she couldn't afford to eat that month). As we explain in Chapter 4, this is a dangerous way to conduct business, not just because you lack the knowledge about rates but you're also letting down the freelance community as a whole. Think about it: if everyone in the freelance world decides to charge low rates then that's what clients become accustomed to. If clients think they can hire someone to do a job for half the money then there's nobody to stop them. So, by charging low rates, you may get more business in but you're also setting low expectations on behalf of your fellow freelancers.

Alarm Bell

Never be tempted to charge below average rates – the freelance community (and your bank balance) is guaranteed to suffer.

You may quote lower rates because you don't have the confidence to charge what you ought to, or are too afraid to charge higher in case another freelancer undercuts you, but there are other reasons why quoting low can have a detrimental effect on your business. So here's the rub: psychologically, people are suspicious of any service that they consider to be 'too cheap'. This means that if you quote a really low rate for a big, complex project then the client will think that there's something wrong with your skills and will, most likely, look for someone else. In most cases, clients want to pay a bit more as they know that quality comes at a price. Charging too low calls your quality of work into question.

So, if you're confused or have doubts about how much to quote for a piece of work, then call your fellow freelancers and ask their advice. Together, you can encourage each other to quote a fair price, even if it means taking a risk and potentially losing a client. And if the client blanches at the thought of paying the price that you quoted, then let them walk away, as there's no reason to do business with someone who doesn't appreciate the skill, talent, and effort that goes into one of the most difficult jobs on earth.

Of course, in the beginning, you'll be so grateful that someone trusts you enough to pay you that you'll accept anything, but as you become more experienced and more confident, and learn to trust in your own abilities, you'll be able to pick and choose, set worthwhile rates, and happily refuse the less lucrative projects.

CASE STUDY: CONTACTS, CONTACTS, CONTACTS

Linda Watson-Brown lives in the north-east of Scotland with her partner and three children. Her books include *The Step Child* and *What Daddy Did* by Donna Ford, *The Pet Whisperer* by Sarah-Jane Le Blanc,

Love Hurts by Jeff Randall, *Casper* by Sue Finden, *Unbreakable* by Lindsey Hunter, and the Grace Monroe crime series: *Dark Angels, Blood Lines, The Watcher,* and *Broken Hearts.* She is represented by Clare Hulton and is currently working on a new crime fiction series as well as continuing to ghostwrite memoirs. You can find out more about her at www.lindawatsonbrown.co.uk.

'I fell into ghostwriting almost by accident – that may, however, be a character trait rather than the hand of fate, given that most of my gainful employment has been acquired in pretty much the same fashion. After spending as long in education as humanly possible, my first grown-up job was as a Politics lecturer at Edinburgh University. The teaching lark continued in various guises for almost ten years until I was offered a position as a columnist at *The Scotsman.* When I finally went freelance, I was lucky enough to be given commissions by pretty much every national newspaper and a batch of women's magazines.

The world of freelancing had been represented as a scary one characterized by lack of security, a constant worry over where the next pay cheque was coming from, and the neverending fear that you'd be unemployable before that day's headlines were dry. That seemed to be pretty much like most jobs if you asked me – I'd never had a contract which couldn't be broken on a month's notice, and I was used to working for unscrupulous employers. Backbiting and nastiness were far more prevalent in academia that I ever found in Fleet Street. So with this completely uncharacteristic Pollyanna approach, I found myself thinking that ghostwriting would be a Jolly Good Idea.

Most journalists will tell you that they frequently interview people who end their story by sighing, "I should write a book". That, despite what you may have read in the *News of the World*, is the sign to make your excuses and leave. However, flushed with yet another batch of pregnancy hormones – always my downfall – when one interviewee did mutter those infamous words, I found myself replying, "Yes, you should". I couldn't really say no when she then asked me to ghost it.

As soon as I stepped into the world of ghostwriting I found that my experience as a freelance journalist was invaluable – not just for the pesky business of actually being able to write, but for the years spent learning the value of contacts and the inability to get embarrassed when contacting complete strangers. I've now been a ghostwriter for five years and I'd give three main bits of advice to anyone considering a similar path: firstly, tell everyone what you do as there is no way of knowing where the next book may appear from; secondly, make as many contacts as possible with support groups, people who say interesting things in newspapers, or those who you just happen to stumble across in day-to-day life; and, finally, ask everyone for advice.

The last point may be the most important of all. When I began this job – and it still seems rather odd to consider it a real "job" as it's generally a fantastic opportunity to do the two things I love best, namely write and have a natter – I had no idea what I was getting into. However, as a former journalist I was used to taking a short cut when there was something I had no knowledge of, and that was simply to ask people who were experts. I don't know whether I was simply lucky enough to only ask the nice ones, or whether everyone in the business is like this, but I found them all universally helpful and supportive. Andrew Crofts, who has pretty much single-handedly invented this entire profession, was beyond kind, always there almost as a blueprint for "what to do" but also with a helping email when things seemed rather tricky. Given his status and work rate, this is quite remarkable, but I genuinely believe that he both made me feel that this was a business which could be cracked, and one which it might be rather fun to be part of.

Andrew was not the only one – I emailed lots of other ghostwriters and found that, universally, they were a grand bunch. Perhaps it is the intrinsic loneliness of the job – after those few days spent interviewing the person who will be the centre of a new book, there are many isolated days spent in the company of nothing more than a laptop and a vast quantity of chocolate. Maybe we're all just desperate to talk to someone who doesn't want to "do" their memoir, but I'd rather believe that we all recognize that there is actually plenty of work to go round, that helping someone else doesn't mean that you yourself lose out, and that we are actually in quite a difficult business which can be softened somewhat by an email or call out of the blue from someone in the same boat.

We all have stories to share – the client who is chatting on *This Morning* about how disciplined they had to be to type 2,000 words a day when you know for a fact that they haven't even read the book you slaved over, the ones who want to discuss their outfit for the launch party at The Ritz when you know they'll never get a contract this side of never-ever, and those who suddenly resent you getting paid at all when this whole writing lark seems so easy for you. But if you can find someone who is up when you're down, who ebbs when you flow, you'll have a much easier time of it.

Contacts, both professional and personal, are the key to this game – and if that sounds as if I'm just opening myself up to dozens of new ghostwriters emailing me with their worries, I'm fine about that – distraction is another major aspect of the job, but that's another essay entirely...*'*

SUMMARY

✓ Get in touch with your frenemies.

✓ Collaborate with your competitors and share information to improve your quality of work.

✓ Research your competition and establish some common interests. This will make it easier to break the ice when you meet them for the first time.

✓ Never be afraid to recommend a trusted colleague to a client in the event you can't take on a piece of work.

✓ Finding a mentor is one of the best ways to learn more and grow your business.

✓ Motivate yourself and others by sharing your experiences with your fellow freelancers.

✓ Swap notes on rates and judge whether you're quoting fairly for a project, or whether you're financially letting yourself (and the freelance community) down.

8

DEALING WITH DIFFERENT
TYPES OF CLIENTS

In this chapter we lead you through the world of client relationship management. It doesn't take a genius to deduce that your ability to please and get on with clients massively influences your success as a freelancer. If you're friendly and professional you're much more likely to build strong working relationships, and it's strong working relationships that equate to more work and more money in the bank.

Every time you work with a client, you have to keep the bigger picture in mind. You don't just want to get through this project; you want the client to decide you're a reliable, efficient, pleasant freelancer who's great at the job, and so hire you again and again and again. (Well, unless the client's a nightmare; we deal with that situation in this chapter too.) Freelancing, after all, is a competitive business. So you need to ensure your clients fundamentally like working with you so they hire you over the other freelancers on their list.

And, of course, it's not just about getting on with people for the sake of building your business. Your job will be a lot easier and a lot more fun if your client relationships are happy, healthy, and mutually fulfilling.

TAKING A PROFESSIONAL APPROACH

As we explain in Chapters 2 and 3, your freelancing is a business, and therefore you must think and behave like a businessperson. And, of course, the cornerstone of successful business is professionalism.

Being professional in your client relationships means being:

- ☐ calm
- ☐ clear
- ☐ communicative
- ☐ fair
- ☐ honest
- ☐ respectful.

Freelancers who pride themselves on being professional in their business dealings are far more likely to succeed. Clients – whether authors or publishers, tiny companies, or vast global organizations – want to work with people who understand the norms and standards expected in working relationships. Professionalism reassures clients that you're an intelligent, experienced, dependable freelancer.

For most people, especially those who've worked in-house in a business environment, being professional comes naturally – it's not something you set out to learn; instead, you pick up the 'rules' of working relationships as you go along. But there are those who miss the boat or become complacent when it comes to building strong, mutually beneficial working relationships.

Here are some examples of being unprofessional – the kinds of actions you want to avoid because they'll damage your business:

- ☐ **Being overly familiar:** Clients may be friendly, but that doesn't mean they want to be your friend. See the following section for more on this.

- ☐ **Being rude:** Clients will be repelled by an abrupt manner ('Where is my cheque?'); a confrontational approach ('So what do you expect me to do about it then?'); an accusatory tone ('But you said I should do that!'); and – heaven forbid – profanity ('The illustration for Chapter 2 was a bloody nightmare!').

☐ **Being too pushy:** Freelancers in publishing aren't pushy salespeople. Say you quoted for a job you'd really like, but the prospective client hasn't hurried to hire you. By all means send a follow-up email politely enquiring where the client is with the job and whether they are interested in working with you, but don't hound the client with calls and emails reiterating how marvellous you and your services are!

☐ **Breaking an agreement/contract:** If you don't stick to agreements, you can't expect your clients to either.

☐ **Coming across as a money-grabber:** For example, if you come down on a client like a ton of bricks because an invoice is slightly overdue, the client is going to feel harassed and annoyed, and is unlikely to want to work with you again.

☐ **Deceiving:** You may get away with little white lies, but big ones will land you in hot water. For example, if you invoice 40 hours' work for a job that took you 12, the client may not confront you over their suspicion that you're overcharging, but they probably won't hire you again.

☐ **Giving up on a project before completion:** It doesn't matter how bored or frustrated you are with a project, you must put your head down and get on with it.

☐ **Gossiping about a client and breaking confidences:** Your reputation is everything for bringing in business, and you can severely damage your image if you bad-mouth clients or share information you should be keeping confidential.

☐ **Missing deadlines:** Unless you have a very good reason and you warn your client in advance that you'll be delivering work late, you really must return work on time (ideally, a little early).

☐ **Not communicating in a timely manner:** Not returning calls or emails (or doing so late) is going to frustrate your client and convey the idea that you aren't really bothered about the client and their project.

☐ **Overruling a client's wishes:** As we explain later in this chapter, freelancers must follow the client's brief to the letter. That's what they're paying you to do, after all!

☐ **Stealing a client's ideas:** For example, you may critique a book that's badly written but has an excellent concept, and be tempted to take the idea of the book and incorporate it into your own novel. Not only is this unfair and dishonest, but stealing ideas can mean violating a person's intellectual property rights (see Chapter 3), and leave you wide open to litigation and with a reputation in tatters.

Alarm Bell

Be especially careful when sending emails, where your tone can be easily misinterpreted.

Remember, if a client finds you to be unprofessional, they simply won't re-hire you. And you can't build a successful freelancing business unless clients come back time and time again.

Are you the consummate professional, or could you improve on your people skills? Adjusting your manner with clients can be a quick, easy, and cost-free way to boost your business.

ACCEPTING AND FOLLOWING THE BRIEF

Freelancers are experienced, skilled, creative people, and we have a wealth of knowledge and ideas that we can bring to a project. Some clients are very happy to defer to the freelancer's expertise, and we love working with clients like these. But many clients prefer to be the boss of a project, and to give the freelancer a clear brief to follow. And because the client is hiring you to perform a service that they define, you must follow the golden rule of business: when it comes to briefs, the client is always right.

Sometimes when you freelance it's very tempting to overstep the mark. For example, Charlie recently edited a business book in which the client insisted she capitalize every occurrence of the words 'Company', 'Organization', and 'Employee'. Charlie very diplomatically explained to the client that the capitalization wasn't necessary (or in fact grammatically correct) and was distracting to the reader, but the client was insistent. So Charlie swallowed her frustration and did exactly as she was asked.

It can also be a very difficult to let go when a client doesn't accept a perfectly good creative piece. For example, a book illustrator may create illustrations that they know, as an artist, are brilliant, but the client demands they make changes that diminish the quality of the art. Similarly, when we write we find it hard when a client pulls apart beautifully crafted writing, failing to see that it's great just as it is. But we have to grit our teeth and make the amendments requested with good grace, because that is our job.

For those freelancers working in editorial services, you may also find yourself struggling to work to brief and instead straying into other services. For example, a proofreader may be tempted to do a little light editing in places and although you may feel that you're being helpful by expanding the scope of your work, you really aren't. Publishers in particular won't thank you for taking it upon yourself to edit a book they hired you to proofread: no doubt they already had the book copy-edited and your interventions are treading on the toes of that editor, who may very well be the same person who's hired you to proofread the book!

Stick to your brief and keep the client happy. Ultimately, you need to let go of your client work and accept that it's not your book and you don't call the shots. In your freelance role you're acting much like a temporary employee, and you need to drill into your mind that your client is in charge of the brief and you must carry out the agreed service – nothing more, nothing less.

Remember, if you aren't happy with what a client wants you to do, the time to deal with this is before you take on the work. If you don't want to follow the client's brief, don't – turn down the project. If you're mid-project and becoming desperately unhappy fulfilling the brief, tell yourself you'll press on and finish this job, but you won't take on another like it.

BEING FRIENDLY – TO A POINT

Different clients expect different levels of personal input. Some of our clients know very little about us and we have a very professional and polite but distant relationship with them. But other clients – particularly authors – like to build a rapport. A bit of banter on email, a 'How was your Christmas?' at the start of a phone call, a chatty lunch meeting now and again – these are all good relationship-building activities. But the professional freelancer must always keep in sight the line between being friendly and over-friendly, and must be careful not to cross over.

Getting the balance right between friendliness and professionalism is really about instinct and carefully reading situations. You should take your lead from the client – responding to their efforts at building rapport. For example, when she returned to work after maternity leave, one of Charlie's publisher clients was keen to hear all about her baby son. Since then, when Charlie works with this client they sometimes share a little about their children in a phone call or email before getting down to business, and this exchange has helped to build a strong working relationship. However, Charlie is careful to limit the personal exchange – she doesn't send the client every new photo of her son or keep up a running commentary of his many antics.

If you start to blur the boundary between client and friend, it complicates the working relationship. How will you assert yourself if a client-who's-now-a-friend messes you about? For example, if the 'client' doesn't pay an invoice, you're going to find it hard to switch from mate to businessperson. You also run the risk of sharing too much about yourself, and thereby damaging your prospects of getting work. You want to come across as unflappable, content, successful, focused, capable – not someone whose partner has cleared out your joint account and run off with your best mate, leaving you broke and broken-hearted.

Alarm Bell

Don't share personal information with clients. Trust us, they really don't want to know about the state of your marriage, your irritable bowel, or your mounting debt. Remember, you have an image to protect.

DEALING WITH DIFFICULT CLIENTS

The vast majority of clients, in our experience, are a pleasure to work with. If you clearly set down terms at the start of a project (see Chapter 3), you're unlikely to encounter problems. But invariably you get the odd one or two clients who present a challenge. That's where it pays to have a thick skin and an assertive approach.

Here are some types of nightmare clients we've come across over the years:

- **Inappropriate:** They cross a line and make you feel uncomfortable. They may ask you personal questions, or share information you really don't want to know. They may call or email too often, or at strange times, and even ask to meet you with an inference that it will be more than a business meeting.

- **Time-wasters:** They mess you about – asking for loads of information and then disappearing into the blue yonder or dithering about on projects that seem to take a lifetime to complete.

- **Unprofessional:** These clients simply haven't a clue how to conduct a professional relationship. They're rude, obnoxious, and overbearing, and working with them brings sheer misery.

Difficult clients can make your life hell, so don't put up with them. You go freelance so you can pick and choose your clients and projects – never lose sight of that freedom. You don't have to work with anyone who mistreats you or makes you feel uncomfortable. Ditch these clients (politely); there are plenty more out there who are great to work with.

 It's often best not to tell a nightmare client exactly why you don't want to work with them any more – you may just awaken the beast!

Although we don't generally advocate lying to clients, telling a partial truth to extricate yourself from a difficult business relationship may be your safest option. You can tell your nightmare client you're sorry but you're unable to work with them because you're busy with other commitments, and you can hold to that approach if they come back further down the road. Just keep being professional, polite, and firm. Usually, the client gets the message and gives up contacting you.

Occasionally, a client can get nasty when you try to cut off from them. Early in her freelancing career, Charlie worked with a one-man publisher who was beyond unprofessional. He started out friendly enough, and she took on a ghostwriting project. But over the following weeks Charlie became steadily more uncomfortable working with the client. He massively moved the goalposts on her project, he rang her constantly to check her progress in the writing, he asked personal questions such as her age and appearance, and he tried to set up a one-on-one meeting in a hotel where he would 'take care of her very well'. Soon Charlie was a jibbering wreck whenever the client called, and she was delighted when the project ended. But two weeks later the client called again with another job. At this point Charlie opted for the white lie of being too busy to take it on, but bizarrely this incensed the client, who began ranting that he would make her name mud in the industry. Charlie remained polite but ended the call, and ignored a couple of subsequent, abusive emails. Happily, she hasn't heard from the client since.

Experiences like these are very rare, but can be difficult to manage when you're working alone as a freelancer. If you're struggling to cope with a difficult client, get advice – talk to friends and family, ask other freelancers for their opinion, and perhaps try a business advice organization such as Business Link.

Also keep in mind that to maintain a level of professionalism, and to ensure your safety, meetings should take place in public places.

Charlie was particularly grateful she'd heeded this advice the day she met a little old lady in a local bookshop's cafe to discuss ghostwriting her memoirs. The meeting started out normal enough – exchanging basics on background, discussing costings, timeframes, and structuring. But after a while, Charlie became increasingly concerned by the client's wandering, staring eyes and the fact she kept muttering into thin air. Finally, the client confided she could see dead people all around who were 'after her', and could Charlie protect her? Needless to say, Charlie had rather enjoyed the film *The Sixth Sense*, but was reluctant to write a book while surrounded by the invisible, malevolent deceased. She gently removed herself from the situation and the potential project. Then she went home very glad she hadn't agreed to the client's original request of meeting at her house, which, the lady had now explained, was home to a particularly evil poltergeist.

It takes all sorts to make a world, and freelancing brings you into contact with a colourful array of people. Just take care to foster healthy, productive relationships and pull away from the tiny minority that makes you feel compromised or concerned.

WORKING WITH DIFFERENT CLIENTS

A freelancer in publishing can work for three different categories of client:

- □ **Book publishers:** From small independents to established publishing houses.

- □ **Authors:** These are individuals whom we often term 'private clients'.

- □ **Businesses:** By this we mean companies and organizations.

Publishers

For most freelancers, publishers are the target client. What freelancer doesn't dream of walking into a bookshop and picking up a title that bears their name on the acknowledgements page? (In fact, we confess we rather enjoy the hunt-for-our-latest-book-to-see-our-name-in-it game!) We want to be part of creating books, and working for publishers brings fulfilment.

Many new freelancers complain that it's hard to break into the publishing industry because it's too cliquey; that this is a world where success comes down to who you know. Although these are unfair generalizations, they do carry a seed of truth.

Networking (creating a network of contacts) is essential in freelancing. Staff in publishing houses want to work with seasoned professionals, which is why they like it when a colleague recommends a reliable and talented freelancer. And because they're a friendly bunch, usually those you work with in publishing are happy to pass on your details should an opportunity arise.

Reputation is important in the industry. The more people you meet in publishing, the more your name travels, and such networking can lead to new clients and projects. Referrals through the publishing network have been a big source of work for both of us. For example, Charlie works for several imprints of one publisher because her initial contact recommended her elsewhere. And when one of Emma's clients, an editor at a publishing house, changed jobs, she was offered projects with the editor's new publisher.

The key to building this network is being good at your job (so clients are happy to refer you), professional, reliable, and, of course, friendly.

You also need to understand the culture you're working within. Book publishing in the UK is an important industry, and it carries a sense of gravitas and history. The freelancer is expected to have an understanding of the industry, and a respect for the business of creating books.

Publishing is an industry that has undergone many changes in recent years, especially in view of developing technology. More so than in business, publishing comprises a blend of those holding on to the past and others looking to the future. Some publishers can only conceive of printed pages; others are exploring e-books. Some keep all elements of the book creation process in-house; others hire various freelancers. Some are progressive and look for ways to cut costs and boost efficiency; others stick to traditional, old-school processes.

For example, for one publishing client Charlie has to copy-edit typeset paper proofs, laboriously marking up using symbols and writing out corrections that someone else then has to key in. Another client simply sends Charlie a Word file, which she copy-edits on screen using the 'track changes' function. You can guess which approach is the more time-consuming, and yet nine times out of ten the traditional publisher's fee is lower than the progressive one's!

Getting on with publishing clients means accepting and respecting the different ways publishers choose to work. It also means keeping up with changes and developments in the industry, so you can keep pace with your clients.

So what do publishers expect of their freelancers? Publishers use freelancers at many different stages in a book's production. We're skilled and experienced, we can be picked up and dropped as needed, and we work out cheaper than hiring in staff.

Publishers expect you to be:

- ☐ commonsensical
- ☐ experienced and skilled
- ☐ friendly
- ☐ honest (especially when it comes to fees)
- ☐ in tune with their style and values
- ☐ open about your availability
- ☐ polite
- ☐ professional
- ☐ punctual.

Most publishers are accustomed to working with freelancers, and have a good understanding what the freelance life is like. (In fact, many of those working in-house in publishing may either have been freelance at some point or are considering it as an option for the future.) So publishing clients do understand things like:

- ☐ theirs isn't your only project
- ☐ you need to be paid on time
- ☐ you need advance warning of a project to fit it into your schedule
- ☐ you're sometimes unavailable during working hours
- ☐ you may not always say yes to a project
- ☐ you're likely to ask plenty of questions.

 Invite your publishing client to give you feedback after a project. This indicates your willingness to learn, and that you'd like to do another project for the client soon in which you can apply your learning.

Authors
Working with authors as opposed to publishers or corporate clients is akin to working with the public as opposed to other businesses. In basic terms, instead of a business-to-business relationship, you're essentially managing a business-to-consumer one.

Authors, then, require expert handling. You have to find the right balance between delivering a professional service and a personal one. Authors expect more from you than publishers and businesses; the relationship is often a little more casual, relaxed, and friendly.

Left to their own devices, authors can cross the line between client and friend (see the earlier section on this). Your job when working with a client is to maintain the business element of the relationship, setting down the framework of the working relationship (such as setting up a project agreement; see Chapter 3) and sticking to it.

The benefit of working with authors is that you have more control in the working relationship. Whereas a publisher may come to you with a project brief, a set fee, and a contract to sign, with an author you often have input into the brief, you set the fee, and you lay down your project terms.

 Even though authors aren't businesses, treat them as if they were. Have complete respect for their projects, even if you think your five-year-old niece could have written a better book!

CASE STUDY: STANDING IN THE AUTHOR'S SHOES

Penny Avis and Joanna Berry are first-time co-authors of the four-book series *Never Mind the Botox*. Here they give their perspective on what authors look for in a freelancer and share their experiences of using a freelance editor to copy-edit and consistency check their books before submitting to publishers and agents.

 ❝As first time authors we were very keen that what we lacked in "editorial pedigree" we'd make up for in professionalism.

Therefore we decided at quite an early stage of writing our book series that we would have the manuscripts professionally proofread by a freelancer. We didn't decide on the extent of that review until we began researching what was on offer to us.

We started with some basic internet searching using the search words like "book proofreading" and "copy-editing". This brought up lots of options, as you might imagine. When looking at the websites, we wanted something that looked professional and clear and easy to understand. We found those sites with a shopping list of the services on offer and some examples (although not pages and pages of dull CVs!) of previous work most helpful. We rejected any websites that looked like cluttered teenage blog pages, that had silly clip art pictures or that were too slow to load due to some fancy front page. We didn't look beyond the websites when we chose – so our message to freelancers would be make sure your site is good!

When it comes to author expectations for the working relationship, we expected the freelancer to know more than us (which isn't hard!) and therefore give clear advice. We had decided early on in our project that "there was no such thing as failure, only feedback" and that we were going to have to get used to taking criticism on the chin: it comes with the territory of being an author. Therefore we really wanted our freelancer to give us very direct and honest feedback, but in a way that didn't leave us too winded!

The freelancer also needed to do a thorough job that was completely in accordance with the brief. Once the service is agreed, you don't want to find the freelancer quibbling about what's in or out of the brief, unless it's clearly a material change by us. Sometimes it's not possible to get your instructions picture perfect, and some degree of common sense and interpretation is always needed. As the saying goes, "What would the man on the Clapham omnibus think was reasonable?"

It's the author's role to set a clear brief at the outset so that the freelancer can get an idea of what the author is looking for. Once the edges of the envelope have been established, then it is perfectly appropriate for the freelancer to use their expertise to guide the author – but probably only within or close to the brief they have been given, at least until they have established a good working relationship with the author, who might then be prepared to accept wider advice or input.

It's also important that the freelancer be professional. The freelancer needs to treat authors in a very similar way to corporate clients or publishers in terms of the content or service they deliver. But the front end, in terms of the service they provide, can be much more informal and personal. This makes the author feel that they have someone on their side in the big bad world of publishing. We wouldn't want to work with anyone who doesn't run their freelancing as a business, as they won't be around for very long! If we have learnt anything, as we make this transition from business-orientated professionals [Penny is an accountant and Joanna is a lawyer] to creative authors, it's that commercial considerations and making money apply equally to whatever field you are in.

Finally, we are very confident (perhaps misguidedly so!) that our book series has commercial potential. That is why we were prepared to invest in having the books professionally copy-edited prior to submitting them. We knew that the publishers would normally do this part themselves, but we wanted to maximize our chances of success by making the product as good as it could be before we sent it. This is perhaps the challenge for freelancers, as others may not have the confidence or the funds to make this sort of investment in their books. We liked having the freedom to make our own decisions on how we went about it and using a freelancer seemed the sensible way forward. We would definitely do it again!'

Businesses

Many freelancers also work outside of publishing, complementing their publishing work with corporate projects, such as writing website copy, indexing reports, or designing and laying out marketing brochures. This can be an excellent way to top up your income, especially because corporate clients tend to pay higher rates than authors and publishers.

Sometimes, corporate work can have a different feel to working for publishers. You may find your corporate clients are more:

☐ **Deadline-driven:** In our experience, business clients often want work returned more quickly than publishers and authors.

☐ **Focused on money:** Money is everything. The business exists to make money. On the one hand, the business is reluctant to pay out money for your services, but on the other hand the work you're hired to do contributes to the money-making aim, however indirectly. The business wants you to deliver value for money, and you're more likely to find corporate clients asking for cost breakdowns and justifications for your fee. However, the business client is also more likely to pay a high fee because they expect service providers to charge at a certain level.

☐ **Managerial:** Project management is big news in business, and we find many businesses like to spend (or waste, depending on your view) plenty of time on the administrative side of a project. Some clients like to have lengthy phone calls, email exchanges, and meetings to discuss the minutiae of a project, rather than just letting you get on with it. This is easily managed, however; you simply factor the toing and froing into your costing for the project.

Business clients want you to be the consummate professional. You have to seamlessly translate and adapt your publishing services for the corporate world. It's with this type of client that you really demonstrate just how business-minded you are.

CASE STUDY: SEEING CLIENTS FROM BOTH SIDES OF THE FENCE

Emma Djonokusumo has been managing publishing clients for many years. After six years as an associate director at a publishing recruitment company JFL Search & Selection, she took the plunge and went freelance. She now works both in-house and remotely for various publishers.

‘Working in the publishing team at recruitment agency JFL was ideal for me as I built my career: I could learn all about the industry, work in a fast-paced, target-driven office environment and make some great contacts. A great learning curve! Six years later, I wondered where the time had gone. I was established as an associate director, had a good track record of successful assignments and enjoyed the diversity that the work offered, but something was missing.

A small voice in my head had become increasingly loud during the year before I decided to finally take the plunge and leave recruitment behind me. I had always gravitated towards any writing, copy-checking or proofreading tasks at JFL and, having met countless candidates over the years enthusing about how much they loved their jobs in publishing, editorial in particular, I started to wonder, could I do this too? It was not an overnight decision to leave my secure job in recruitment and jump into the unknown. It took a lot of soul searching, planning and research, but the notions in my head had become more and more fleshed out and I decided to go for it. I'd had six great years in a company in which I had grown professionally but it was time for a change, pure and simple. It was time to be brave. So I jumped . . .

The transition between employment and freelancing was an interesting time. There was the absence of a regular pay cheque. No. More. Salary. Talk about motivation! And then there was working from home. Would I miss the buzz of an office? Would I crave company? Would I go mad and start talking to myself (or the cat)?

But an easier transition for me was going from being an employee to a businesswoman with clients. That's where my background has been a real benefit.

Working in a recruitment agency, or agency side in any discipline, is the best way to learn how to put yourself in other people's shoes. Recruitment is expensive; there are hundreds of recruiters out there: some excellent, some cowboys. Your reputation as a recruiter spreads quickly (and never more quickly than if you do a bad job). Mud sticks, as they say, so it's imperative that every encounter you have with a client is as professional and positive for that client as possible.

The cycle is simple: the client has a problem: he's short-staffed, pressured and overworked. As a recruiter, you solve that problem. You find him staff and ease the pressure. The client doesn't need to know how you do it; he just wants results in the shortest, least complicated way possible. You are his eyes and ears in the industry, you provide him with a solution and you make it look effortless. He doesn't need to hear about the research, the advertising space negotiation and the countless interviews you go through to make a shortlist of three CVs to show him. But you go through this process and you deliver a solution with grace, good humour and always with the attitude that nothing is too much trouble. He changes the brief at the eleventh hour? You start again. You let the candidates down gently, you re-write the job ad, you re-interview and you submit three different CVs, hopefully ones that will meet his brief.

And while you're doing all this, you have another 20 similar clients, all needing to be your priority, your first phone call. Everyone's problem is the biggest and everyone needs someone in place "yesterday". If I learned anything from the recruitment years it was how to juggle. And well.

How does this translate to freelancing? Well, understanding what clients needed from me then as their recruiter, I would say very similar things are required, namely:

- ☐ consistency
- ☐ quality
- ☐ reliability
- ☐ results.

Be the freelancer they call when they're let down at the eleventh hour because their usual editor has had a personal crisis. *Be* the person who will deliver quality results consistently.

You work for different clients. Each client has different deadlines, different house styles and different ways they prefer to work with you. You need to remember these differences, appreciate them and adapt to them. You are a chameleon but as far as they are concerned, you are an extension of their business; they don't know who else you work for, nor do they really care. The client is king and diplomacy, patience and a very good memory will get you far.

Also, good training I gained in recruitment was the habit of always trying to meet people you do business with. Put a face to a name, build a personal relationship beyond email and make sure you're front of mind when a client needs help. Having made good contacts in the publishing industry before going freelance helped immensely, but it was also reassuring to know that I could approach a new client "cold" and didn't suffer from feelings of rejection if they didn't come back to me or said they didn't need my services. Having now met the clients I worked with at the beginning of my freelancing, they pass me more work and have even recommended me to others – the best result, and compliment of your work, you can ask for.

Right now, I'm in the fortunate and very interesting position of being both temporary in-house staff for a charity and working freelance from home. Having been approached to cover a position in a charity while they recruited someone full time, I jumped at it. However, I made sure that they could accommodate my established and ongoing freelance commitments as this was my priority and I hadn't been looking to return to an in-house role.

Working part time in an office after nearly eight months away is proving beneficial on several levels: it reassures me that I can, indeed, still interact with people in a professional office environment and multi-task, learn new systems and pick up new skills quickly; it is a nice balance of commuting, working a "regular" day and still having time to honour freelance work and, of course, it's a salary again! It hasn't made me think I'd like to return to an office full time and it *has* confirmed that I made the right decision in going freelance in the first place.

I would recommend, in the early days, working in-house, even for a few weeks/a month here and there. I don't see it as a distraction but as additional research into my ultimate, idyllic working pattern and future freelance career. It is really highlighting the decisions you've made and there is always room for new skills, new contacts and a new perspective. '

SUMMARY

Here are some ways you can build strong, mutually-beneficial working relationships:

✓ Always strive to be professional in your working relationships.

✓ Avoid being rude, pushy, or dishonest at all costs.

✓ Let go of being an 'artiste' in your work; save that attitude for your own creative projects.

✓ Follow the brief to the letter.

✓ Take care not to be over-friendly with clients.

✓ Protect yourself from difficult clients, and refuse to work with someone if you aren't comfortable.

✓ Make a positive reputation for yourself in the publishing industry.

✓ Attune yourself to publishers' individual styles.

✓ Find the right balance between a personal service and a professional one with private clients.

✓ Be prepared for a shift in pace and working style when taking on business projects.

9
EXPLORING ALL AVENUES

Have you secretly yearned to be an editor rather than a proofreader? Or perhaps you come from an editorial background and would love to become an author? You might think making the transition from one area in freelancing to another is impossible – it's not. The beauty of freelancing is that it gives you the freedom to explore different roles and broaden your skillset. You just have to go about it in the right way.

Over the years, we've both delved into all sorts of different freelance roles. Emma started off as a copy editor, proofreader and book critiquer before moving into writing and is now a full-time ghostwriter and author in her own right. However, she hasn't turned her back on the editing side, and still likes to take on the odd bit of work, especially during those scary dry periods! Charlie primarily works as a high-level editor but also does her fair share of writing.

WHICH IS THE BEST ROLE FOR YOU?

With the number of different freelance roles out there, it can be difficult to know which ones are right for you. Don't worry if you've started off in one area and then wish to change to another; as long as you market the transition in the right way, then you'll still be in a good position to attract new business. The great thing about being a freelancer is that there's no requirement to pigeon-hole yourself into one specific area, and there's no stubborn boss around refusing to let you try out a new role. Making the change is totally up to you, but it takes courage, determination, and a fair degree of confidence.

So, as an example, the following is a step-by-step summary (warts and all) of how Emma made the transition from editor and proofreader, to ghostwriter and author:

☐ Emma quits marketing executive job at a fancy US investment bank, and sets up a copy-editing and proofreading business (even though she really wants to be a writer).

☐ Emma designs her own website (amateurish is an understatement), sorts out business cards, and goes along to every publishing event under the sun, promoting herself as copy editor and proofreader (even though she still really wants to be a writer).

☐ Work starts dribbling in, a slow trickle at best, and while Emma doesn't mind editing and proofreading, she isn't exactly in love with it (can you guess why?).

☐ By some miracle, an author and journalist asks Emma to help him with his latest manuscript, and she ends up ghosting the whole thing for him (she's never been so happy!).

☐ The chance ghosting project gives Emma the confidence in her writing skills she needs to believe in herself.

☐ Emma contacts publishers who are willing to hire her to write book jackets, book introductions, and so on.

☐ Emma gets in touch with other ghosts who are happy to pass her some work.

☐ Emma hires a web design company to create a new and improved website (www.emmamurray.net), gets new business cards printed up, and launches herself as a ghostwriter.

☐ Emma gets a steady flow of ghostwriting work in and successfully gets a number of books commissioned with various different publishers.

☐ A major publisher commissions Emma as an author to write a business book about a top entrepreneur.

☐ Being aware of the curse of the freelance famine, Emma still offers other services alongside her ghostwriting, including consultancy services that involve book critiquing, proposal writing, and rewrites and restructures on manuscripts.

Emma's transition from one area to another took about two years, and it wasn't easy. However, she could have done things differently and speeded up the process. So here are some tips about how to make a smoother and more successful transition within the freelance publishing world:

☐ Decide exactly what sort of services you'd like to offer.

☐ Do your research: use your contacts and get in touch with other freelancers who carry out that role, and find out as much about it as you can.

☐ Educate yourself as much as you can. Take courses, attend seminars, read books on the subject. Clients will expect you to be an expert in your field.

☐ Once you've made your decision, sort out your website, business cards, and so on, and get the message out there.

☐ Never burn your bridges completely. Offer your new skills as an addition to your services, rather than scrapping your previous services altogether.

☐ Keep taking on the 'old' work while you're waiting for the 'new' work to come in – you never want to be in a position where you don't have any work at all!

□ Once you have a steady stream of 'new' work coming in, and you've successfully built up a good reputation with your clients, then you can pick and choose the work you want to do – every freelancer's dream!

□ Most importantly: be brave, be confident, be patient, and have faith in your talent!

CHOOSING YOUR FREELANCE ROLE

There are lots of freelance roles out there to explore. You can specialize in one area, or combine a few skills, or expand your business further down the road by moving into a totally different area – it's totally up to you! However, be careful about marketing yourself as a jack-of-all-trades, as your clients might be suspicious of someone who looks like they're juggling too much, and might think that you won't have the time to focus on their projects. We suggest advertising yourself with three to four skills, at most.

The following is a list of freelance roles you might be interested in pursuing that we've done ourselves (proofreading, editing, critiquing, ghosting, and so on) and feel we have enough knowledge and experience to share with you. However, at one time or another we've come into contact or worked with freelancers in different fields in publishing, such as graphic design, project management, production services, typesetting, illustration, research, indexing, and translation. We're not experts in these areas, so in the following section we call on the real professionals to give you the lowdown on some of these roles.

Proofreading

Are you one of those people who's driven insane by typos in the newspaper? Do you secretly yearn to take a marker pen to a local shop sign that says 'Freds Fish Shop', and correction fluid to a menu that offers 'Sweat and Sour Chicken'? If so, within you may beat the heart of a proofreader.

Understanding the job

Proofreading is one of the final stages in a book's editorial process. To ensure effective proofreading, the book should be in pretty good shape when it arrives on the proofreader's desk, having been professionally copy-edited and typeset beforehand. Thus, the book proofreader focuses on spotting those odd mistakes that have slipped through the net, rather than being inundated with a sea of errors that overloads the eyes, making it much harder to spot each and every problem.

Proofreaders' dos and don'ts

Proofreaders look at the main body of the book, as well as prelims and endlims (the first and last pages of the book), indexes, and references. A proofreader looks at two areas as they read:

- ☐ **Accuracy:** Corrects errors in spelling, punctuation, and grammar, catching all misspellings, spotting a misplaced apostrophe, and sorting dodgy verb agreements.

- ☐ **Consistency:** Brings the text neatly into line, ensuring a consistent style is applied in areas such as capitalization, italicization, hyphenation, punctuation, and spelling styles. Elements such as numbers, abbreviations, titles, bulleted and numbered lists, and tables and figures must adhere to one global style.

It's *not* part of the proofreader's job to:

- ☐ **Improve the text:** Proofreaders don't rewrite clumsy sentences, improve flow, break down over-long paragraphs, or suggest that a plot has lost pace. These are elements that editors look at (see later sections).

☐ **Lay out the text:** Some proofreaders lay books out for their clients. This is design work, and is an additional service – not an integral part of the proofreader's role.

☐ **Fact check:** Proofreaders often check that details like web addresses are correct, but they don't generally check the accuracy of information included in the book. So a proofreader isn't responsible for checking the dates in a sentence such as, 'Henry VIII was born on 28 June 1491 in Greenwich'. However, proofreaders are intelligent and have a good deal of common sense, so they will flag an obvious error such as, 'Henry VIII had 16 wives'.

On-screen versus paper proofs

These days, many clients ask you to proofread on-screen, using the 'track changes' feature of Microsoft Word so that your changes are visible. When Charlie proofreads, this is by far her preferred way of working, because it's quick, easy, and efficient.

But some publishers are still of the old school mentality, and require proofreaders to mark up paper proofs of the typeset book using the British Standard proofreading marks. The proofs are then passed back to the typesetter, who inputs the changes.

In paper proof work, a proofreader's role encompasses checking the typesetter's work. For example, the proofreader may check that all the edits on the copy editor's marked-up proofs have been carried out correctly in these new proofs. He or she also looks at elements such as page numbering, running heads, and whether words have been split sensibly over a line or page.

If you do proofread paper proofs, remember to charge the client for your postage and print costs.

Becoming a proofreader

Far too many people think they can proofread. We've lost track of how many authors have been staggered by the number of corrections we've made to their books – they thought they were pretty good at proofreading, but the truth is, proofreading involves a lot more than just spotting the odd typo.

Proofreading requires natural ability – intelligence, a perfectionist approach, an instinctive feel for language, an eye for detail, an analytical mind, an ability to notice that the discrepancy between 'realize' on page 12 of a book and 'realise' on page 212.

You can teach yourself how to proofread by using books on the subject, but the easiest way to learn is on a training course – either distance learning, at a training centre, or in-house at work.

Alarm Bell

Beware of companies advertising proofreading courses that promise you can make £30k per annum doing this job thanks to their £80 course. These companies will not give you the calibre of training you need to be a professional proofreader.

Finding work

Type 'proofreader' into a UK search engine and you'll get a good idea of the type of competition you face. Proofreading is a very popular service offered by freelancers.

The most experienced proofreaders command the highest fees and work for the higher level clients – the big publishing houses and published authors. But work is available for newbie freelance proofreaders as well, as long as you're not fussy over the type of material you read at first.

 It's not just publishers and authors who hire proofreaders. You can also market your proofreading service to charities, companies, and organizations, and you may well earn better money working with such clients.

Freelancers who build up enough experience and a strong client base can work full time as proofreaders. But because proofreading is the most straightforward of the editorial services, you can never charge the highest rates for the work. That's why many freelance proofreaders also offer complementary services, such as editing, and only proofread for part of their income.

Copy-editing

Many proofreaders itch to do more to books – to go a step beyond correcting the text and move into improving it. Whereas a proofreader merely reads proofs, checking for mistakes that have slipped through the net, a copy editor edits a book, which means they go much further in making changes.

Understanding the job

Like a proofreader, a copy editor looks at accuracy and consistency in a book. But, in addition to these basic checks, they also work to improve the text. Depending on need and requirement, here are just some of the elements of a book upon which a copy editor may focus:

- ☐ brevity
- ☐ capitalization
- ☐ clarity

- ☐ headings
- ☐ italicization
- ☐ length of sentences
- ☐ paragraphing
- ☐ repetition
- ☐ use of bullets and numbered lists
- ☐ use of punctuation
- ☐ vocabulary.

Knowing where the line is

Of all the services freelancers can provide in the publishing industry, copy-editing is one of the trickiest to master because the nature of the work isn't set in concrete. The client may require a very light, restrained copy-edit in which you simply improve the odd clumsy sentence or, alternatively, a thorough, intensive, roll-your-sleeves-up-and-make-changes-all-over edit. A copy editor's job is to understand exactly what level of edit the client requires, and deliver the work exactly to brief. As we explain in Chapter 8, a freelancer must always follow the client's instructions.

Sometimes, this means you 'under edit' text that really does require more intensive editing, and that can be pretty frustrating, especially if – like us – you take pride in your work. When a client commissions you to do a light edit only, that's exactly what you have to do – even if you can see areas that could be further improved.

Keeping to editorial guidelines, however, doesn't preclude intelligent copy-editing, by which we mean discussing with the client any major issues you can see that fall outside the remit of your edit. For example, if you notice content that's on a shaky legal footing or you suspect is plagiarizing other published text, the client will usually be delighted to hear about it. Clients appreciate perceptive copy editors who flag up important issues. Laying out exactly when and how a copy editor should do this is impossible: intelligent copy-editing is about intuitively adapting to each client's style and knowing where the boundaries lie.

In their edit, the copy editor must also be careful not to cross the line from necessary editing into trampling on the author's individual style. You must be a chameleon – matching your style to the author's as you work, respecting their creativity, and taking care not to tread on their toes by imposing your personal preferences and style on the text.

Specialized copy-editing

You may also consider offering these specialized copy-editing services:

- ☐ **Plain English editing:** This involves making text as clear, concise, and simple as possible. You'll need to learn the ins and outs of this communication style – either by buying a book or going on a Plain English Course.

- ☐ **Technical editing:** If you have a background in a technical field – science, maths, education, the medical profession, for example – you can offer your services as a technical editor. Technical editors can make good money working with academic publishers. For example, we know a former primary school teacher who now makes a comfortable income editing teaching materials on a freelance basis.

- ☐ **US/UK editing:** Those with experience of both UK and US English can 'translate' text for clients between the two. Be warned: you must have significant experience of your non-native language to successfully carry out this service. Having a passion for US-authored crime novels isn't enough to equip you for the translation; you need to have studied the opposing language and immersed yourself in it (as Charlie did while at university in the States, for example).

Becoming a copy editor

More so than for a proofreader, a copy editor needs to be experienced and a good writer themselves. You can't expect to offer your services as a professional copy editor if all that qualifies you to do the job is a love of books. You need to have a natural feel for language: an innate understanding that a sentence is too long or a word is repeated too often.

The majority of copy editors are also trained for the job – whether in-house, on a course, or self-taught with books. Without training, you won't have a clue what to do with your first book, because there's a lot more to copy-editing than simply tidying language. For example, if you intend to work with publishers, you'll need to learn how to copy-edit paper proofs.

 One of the best ways to learn to copy-edit is to review material that a professional copy editor has worked on. You can find examples in books, and plenty on good training courses, and if you work for a publisher as a proofreader and are keen to progress you can ask for examples of copy-editing to learn from.

Finding work

Alas, not as many clients realize the need for copy-editing as they do proofreading. Too many authors hire Charlie only to proofread their 'finished' manuscript, when in fact the book needs a thorough copy-edit.

Some authors, though, do understand that copy-editing is as essential a part of preparing a book for publication as proofreading. And, of course, publishers routinely hire copy editors to tidy up authors' rough manuscripts and bring them into line with the house style.

Private clients don't always realize the need for copy-editing, so part of your challenge is convincing an author that they need more than a proofread. You can do this by offering a sample edit, so they can see how copy-editing works.

Publishers can also be reluctant to take on new copy editors. Unless you're an experienced copy editor, you'll usually be started on proofreading projects, and then moved on to copy-editing if you show promise. The bad news is, it may be harder to get copy-editing work than proofreading. However, on the plus side, copy-editing pays more, and once a publisher sees you can edit well, they're likely to keep you on the list for this work.

 If you lack experience in copy-editing, start off trying to gain experience as a proofreader. Once you have a strong background and have honed your skills, you can move up the ladder to editing.

High-level editing

Not for the faint-hearted, this is the level of work that many in-house editors at publishing houses perform. These are the people who pull a book together, who see all the problems in a book and dive in to sort them out, who contribute the most to making the book a good one.

Understanding the job

Some publishers lump all types of editing into the category of 'copy-editing'. We don't think this is a useful practice. 'Copy-editing' as a service doesn't quite cover the whole spectrum of editorial services. Copy-editing, as its name suggests, focuses on the copy – the text – whereas a higher level of editing may look at the structure, the plot, or the suitability of the book for the target audience.

We prefer to separate out the higher level of editing that goes beyond the simple copy-edit and requires much more experience and expertise. This high-level editing may include:

- □ **Book management:** You act as a project manager, liaising with the author, designer, typesetter, and publisher, choosing artwork, arranging permissions, and managing other freelancers.

- □ **Development editing:** You help develop an author's book, either as they write or afterwards. You may look at aspects such as overall structuring, chapter structures, plot, setting, characterization, pace, author voice, dialogue, and description, to name but a few.

- □ **Rewriting:** You assume the author's style and rework weak areas of a book yourself.

Becoming a high-level editor

Only the most experienced and able editors are hired to do high-level editorial work, and most editors working at this level are also writers. Your path to becoming a freelance high-level editor will either be by gaining experience in a similar role in-house, working your way up the editorial ranks from proofreader upwards, or coming in at the top as an accomplished writer.

Whereas publishers are generally happy to hire copy editors and proofreaders to work on books with minimal support – perhaps just a house style guide to work from – they usually take much more interest in what a high-level editor does, at least until you prove your ability. For example, one of Charlie's clients took her through a training and induction period before sitting back and letting her get on with projects.

Finding work

This is very demanding work, and therefore many publishers prefer their in-house team to take care of it. But you do find some publishers that outsource elements of high-level editing. And, occasionally, you come across authors who are humble enough to accept they need such support, and who are prepared to pay a fee that far exceeds that of proofreading and copy-editing.

For book management, you need to have a good understanding of the industry and a proven ability to project manage. For development editing and rewriting, you need a solid background as a copy editor and/or writer.

Critiquing

Are you one of those people who loves to analyse? For example, are you an armchair critic – do you enjoy unpicking the good and the bad in a book, and deciphering the magic formula, the X factor, that makes a particular book amazing? If you're also a good writer, you've got the basic skills for book critiquing.

Understanding the job

A book critique – also known as a manuscript assessment or appraisal – reviews a completed book. In a nutshell, the critique outlines what's good and bad in a book, and whether or not it's of a publishable standard.

A critique may cover elements such as:

- ☐ characterization
- ☐ genre/readership
- ☐ plot development
- ☐ readiness for publication
- ☐ structure
- ☐ writing style.

When you critique a book, you read the book carefully and then stand back and look at the bigger picture. Then – in a sensitive manner – you give the client your honest opinion of the book.

Critiques are commissioned by authors who are looking to send their book to agents/publishers. They want an expert opinion on whether they have a shot at publication, and what elements of their book require development.

Agents also sometimes use freelancers for critiquing. The professionals who read submitted manuscripts ('the slush pile') and decide which are worthy of consideration are called 'readers'. When the reader comes across a book of interest, they write an appraisal for the agent that sums up the strong and weak areas.

Publishers don't hire freelancers to critique books because they don't need to: the books they publish are either commissioned or have been approved by the commissioning team, who do their own appraisals.

Critiquing books

Clients will expect you to have a wealth of experience in publishing and in working with books. You're likely to be a writer yourself, or perhaps have a background in bookselling, and have an excellent understanding of which books get published in the current market. You should also be well-read in the genre within which the book falls, so you can assess the book against its competition.

This isn't a service a proofreader or copy editor is equipped to offer; you need to have a higher level of experience and expertise.

Finding work

If you have the background and skills to offer book critiquing as a service, you'll have to compete with other successful freelancers and manuscript assessment agencies to get clients. Few authors have the courage, humility, and bank balance to commission a book critique, and agents do not have frequent vacancies for readers, so there are very few book critique clients to share among professionals offering the service.

It's unlikely you'll be able to make a living solely through book critiquing, as with many of the more niche editorial services, but it's a service you can offer alongside others that are more in demand and thus more lucrative.

Reviewing

If you're a bookworm who's well-read and enjoys appraising reading material, book review work may be right up your street. Imagine getting paid just to do what you love – reading books!

Understanding the job

Book reviewers read books and then write a short review that comprises a summary of the story and an opinion on the book. The review may be for a publisher, a website, a magazine, a newsletter, or a newspaper.

For some reviews, experience in the subject matter isn't essential – for example, you don't need to be an expert in relationships to decide whether a book on finding your soulmate is well-written, useful, and inspiring. However, to review most books you need to be well-read within the genre, and you may need to have a background that equips you to assess the book as an informed reader. For example, a crime fiction reviewer needs to have read plenty of crime books – particularly bestselling titles in the last few years; and a parenting book reviewer needs to be a parent, or at the very least have worked extensively with parents and children.

Becoming a book reviewer

All you need is to be able to write, to convey opinions, and to summarize effectively. You don't need formal training or qualifications, but you're going to have to convince clients that you're suitably experienced to do the job.

Finding work

Very few freelancers work as book reviewers, particularly as their core specialism. Not only is this work poorly paid – we know of magazines paying as little as £30 for a review – but there simply isn't much available.

Those who review books are experts in the book's subject matter, published authors, or journalists from magazines and newspapers. No freelance proofreader will be hired to write a book review for the *Guardian*. However, freelance publishing professionals may be able to secure reviewing work for their local paper or magazine.

Of course, doing some book reviews may be a good way to improve your website and your image as a book expert, and you may decide to do this work as a means to building your business, alongside your other services. But very few freelancers will find enough reviewing work to make this a main service.

Ghostwriting

The act of ghostwriting involves writing books or any piece of literature (magazine or news articles, financial reports, and so on) on behalf of someone else.

Understanding the job

Most people associate ghostwriting with celebrity culture and it's true that, at one time or another, footballers, film stars, pop singers, business moguls, gangsters, and royalty have all used the services of ghostwriters. Contrary to popular belief, however, it's not just the Katie Prices of this world who hire ghostwriters to pen their novels on their behalf, and you don't have to be famous to use one. Your client could be a businessman who's simply too busy and exhausted to sit down and write every night; or he might not be confident in his own writing style or grasp of the English language. Similarly, your client might be an academic who's a good writer but doesn't have the appropriate writing style to appeal to a larger audience, outside the field of academia.

So, the ghostwriter might have many different sorts of clients from all walks of life: academic, business, and celebrity, for starters. Each client and project is unique and must be treated as such. As a ghostwriter you must have a clearly defined process from the beginning of each project.

Becoming a ghostwriter

Ghostwriting is a difficult job, and it's not surprising that there are so few ghosts out there. It is one of those jobs that you have to be completely in love with to make it a success. So, how do you know that ghosting is for you? The following are some essential skills, qualities and values you need to be a talented ghostwriter:

☐ an excellent command of the English language

☐ a passion for writing and reading

☐ curiosity and a willingness to learn, study, and research other subjects

☐ an ability to get on with people from different walks of life and different backgrounds

☐ a flexible lifestyle: clients might need you to travel, and sometimes at a moment's notice

☐ an open mind even when you disagree with the client on a certain matter

☐ excellent planning with impeccable project management skills

☐ a good business mind and head for figures (when pricing a project)

☐ a tough shell: rejection from publishers can be hard to take for both you and your client and it's important not to let emotions cloud your judgment

☐ an ability to accept that you might not be credited for your work

☐ an ability to be discreet, reliable, trustworthy, and professional, at all times.

Finding work

The best way to get started as a ghost is to contact other ghosts, who will be more than happy to give you advice, pass you on work, or refer you to other clients whose projects they don't have time to take on. You can also follow the advice we provide in Chapter 5 on marketing your business, setting up a website, creating business cards, and attending publishing events. It's also important to contact publishers and literary agents who are often on the lookout for ghostwriters to pen a book or two on behalf of their clients.

It takes time to build up a reputation as a ghostwriter, so it pays to be patient. However, once you really get going and your reputation builds, you'll be able to pick and choose which books you want to work on, and you'll probably find yourself turning down work!

OVER TO THE EXPERTS

As promised, we've consulted professional freelancers in the following roles to give you the best idea of what other freelance roles are all about.

Freelance copywriter

Mark Johnson is the Director of MJCopywriting Limited (www. mjcopywriting.co.uk; tel: 01728 684326; email: markg_johnson @yahoo.co.uk).

'Freelance copywriters are persuasive writers. They use the written word to communicate ideas and messages that encourage the reader to take an intended action (buy a product, enter a competition, vote for a political party, and so on). Copywriters tend to fall into two broad areas of specialization: long or short copy. I am fortunate enough to work in both; fortunate, because they both offer their own pleasures.

Long copy includes case studies, brochures, journalism, and other examples of extended pieces of writing. Short copy includes advertisements, direct mail, and so on. They require a slightly different approach and thought process but they share the same starting points. The copywriter must understand the client's communication goals, the subject they are writing about, and the audience the message is intended to persuade. Experience can be helpful, but in most cases it can only be understood through in-depth research before the writing begins.

Working freelance in any field requires prior experience. I worked for 15 years in educational publishing and journalism. My background as a magazine editor was the more useful when deciding to work for myself. Freelance journalism is a well-trodden path and I had many fine freelance journalists as contacts from whom I drew both inspiration and solid advice. But even with these clear advantages, the freelance decision remained a courageous one. Most people, given the choice between leaving a full-time job with a clear career structure and working for themselves, lose confidence and stay where they are; even if their job makes them miserable. So before making the leap I conducted market research. My concern was whether or not I would be unemployed rather than self-employed for the first three months. But there are many potential business opportunities for the freelance copywriter in publishing when first setting out. Once you start exploring them they become increasingly exciting.

The most daunting part of working freelance is finding work. Some freelance copywriters claim to have won business through networking and social events. I can't vouch for that. For example, I would never have encountered my clients based in Switzerland, the USA, Egypt, or Hong Kong in this way. They came via my website. And so the web has been the most powerful tool for finding new clients. The best source of work, however, is existing clients. And you can only grow this business if you supply consistently strong work. Like a jobbing actor, you are only as good as your last job.

Freelance copywriting is a solitary occupation. If you like mixing with colleagues, you won't enjoy the freelance life. However, if you love writing, working alone means you can immerse yourself and achieve a lot. You sometimes have no work. This can be terrifying for the first few years. But work always turns up. It took me five years to see these 'quiet days' as an opportunity to take a break. The buzz of winning new business is addictive. When a new or existing client offers you a new project, you just want to punch the air! It's a thrill I would find hard to replace. '

Freelance desk researcher

Simone Apel has run Publisher's Research Services (PResS) since 2001, providing research, fact checking, and web research training courses for book publishers, editors, journalists, and authors. She studied for an Information Studies masters degree at London Metropolitan University while working for a multinational book publisher's archive and information service. Five years after developing a commercial information brokerage for publishers at the University of Buckingham, she started out as a freelancer. PResS has clients all around the world from the UK to the United States and Australia, from book publishers and journalists to authors and academics. (www.press4research.co.uk)

'If since childhood you've soaked up knowledge like a sponge and your mum had a job prising your head out of encyclopaedias, then perhaps the job of desk researcher is for you. At grass roots level you need to excel at two things – lateral thinking and an obsessive attention to detail. Couple this with a delight in anything that resembles detective work and you have some idea of a desk researcher's lot. It's no good being a web geek – you don't only need to be experienced in web searching and evaluating websites to pick out the junk from the jewels, you also need a good knowledge of libraries, information database tools, and research resources around the world. The job involves some travelling to libraries and information centres, chatting up fellow information professionals in order to acquire information, and lots of sitting at a desk! Sounds fun? It is!

An average week as a desk researcher might involve being asked to research any subject on a variety of levels, from primary to academic, and from curriculum subjects to political issues, so you have to be prepared to swot up on subjects you know nothing about. You might spend one day fact-checking a school textbook on environmental issues, then the next visiting the British Library for newspaper articles. On day three you may be doing a spot of genealogy research for an autobiography, while searching the General Register Office database for birth certificates. On day four you may be back to fact-checking English language teaching texts and then hunting down statistics on deaths in civil wars on day five. Other research might involve choosing books and websites for a bibliography, tracking down copyright holders, providing financial accounts for a business customer, and searching news databases for a journalist.

Research is a key element of most degrees, especially higher degrees, so a degree in something academic is a good start. Or take my route via a postgraduate diploma and/or masters degree in Information Studies (think librarianship in the 21st century!). This teaches you in-depth research skills, library reference and information database skills, and using the web as a research tool. You should gain the skills to research any subject under the sun, as well as your specialist degree subject.

Being a desk researcher isn't particularly easy to get into, as many editors and authors do their own, so you'll need to prove yourself first by offering some free research, which will hopefully persuade them that you can save them time and money in the long term. Expect to charge the NUJ's going rate for freelancers: £20–30 an hour (www.londonfreelance.org/feesguide). '

Freelance permissions editor

Jackie Newman has worked as a freelance permissions editor for over eight years, and has extensive experience in children's and educational publishing. Further details can be found on www.press4research.co.uk/ unlimitpages.asp?id=42.

'A permissions editor is someone who researches and clears permissions on behalf of publishers or authors. My job involves tracking down the copyright holder/s and requesting permission to include material in the new title. Usually, I write to the copyright holder to obtain a licence to use the material, agree fees, and prepare the acknowledgements section for the new component. Depending on the rights requested for the new book/CD/website there may be more than one copyright holder so you may have to go through the process of searching and writing a number of times to obtain a single permission.

A lot of research is involved and it's not always easy to track down the correct copyright holder. Authors and publishers may not always give you adequate information so be prepared to be a hunter-gatherer! Your research might be carried out online, in libraries, via telephone, or email. I have collected, in the course of my career, a wide collection of books and anthologies to help with the job.

My clients vary from authors to small companies and large publishing houses. They may ask me to clear permissions for anything from a novel, a poetry anthology, story anthology, academic reader, to a textbook. I find that these days the jobs are getting increasingly complex with less and less time allowed for clearance. This often means that I end up working long hours and weekends to meet very tight deadlines.

Before I became a freelance permissions editor, I worked in publishing for 12 years. This gave me the general knowledge, contacts, and experience to set up on my own. This job is not for everyone: you need to be able to work under pressure, to tight deadlines, and keep neat paperwork and a paper trail to show how you have contacted/attempted to contact the copyright holders.

The salary varies but it is in the region of £15–22 per hour. Do bear in mind that out of this comes your tax money, paper, ink, envelopes, files, and so on. Like many freelance roles, it can take a while to earn a decent wage until you get established, but if you are determined enough you will get there!'

Freelance graphic designer

Adrian Powell is a freelance graphic designer for scientific and medical publishers in Oxford and London. He can be contacted through his website www.ar-design.co.uk.

'I am one half of two freelance graphic designers working under the banner of A&R Design for, predominantly, scientific and medical publishers. In many ways the world of freelance graphic design is a very different beast to the one I started out in almost 17 years ago. Computer-based image manipulation and desktop publishing was in its early days, but because I came from an electronic music background, I was able to harness these new tools with relative ease.

For the first few years, this apparent visual alchemy brought us a fair amount of work, together with an equal amount of distrust from traditional printers, in-house design departments, and old-school illustrators. As the technology progressed, so did its availability and more competition emerged as a result. In order to stay on top of the game, I had to make the most of my skills as a freelancer: to deliver a project to the satisfaction of the client, on budget, always on time, and, in the case of graphic design, make the product look better than it actually is.

I had hoped that becoming a freelancer would allow me to set working times, enabling me to pursue other interests, but I soon realized that, in publishing, your working rhythms are dictated by those of your clients. There is definitely work flexibility to be enjoyed, but you need the discipline to work on your own to take advantage of it. In publishing, deadlines are everything, and as a freelancer you are the one whose time is going to be squeezed first and generally the most. Editors will always need more time, and ink is always going to need a set time to dry. However, if you manage to get your clients out of tight corners, while retaining a sense of humour (essential) and maintaining a certain standard of work, then you're halfway there.

Without a fellow freelancer to bounce ideas off and share woes with I never would have made it this far, so get to know other people in your field, not only for your mental health, but so you have someone who can take your overflow work and vice versa. Don't undersell yourself – a cheap quote undermines the quality of your work and could become a millstone further down the line. Finally, if you decide you do have what it takes to be a freelancer, then quite simply go for it. Job done. '

Freelance translator

Ursula Meany Scott is a freelance translator with a background in literature. She specializes in translating from French and Spanish into English, and has translated a novel by French author, Claude Ollier, together with numerous shorter works for the Dalkey Archive Press. She can be contacted at ursulameanyscott@gmail.com.

'A freelance translator requires several skills in order to run a successful business, amongst which are: a high level of written proficiency in the mother tongue; a solid comprehension of at least one other language; a meticulous mind coupled with a natural attention to detail; the self-discipline to allow for efficient time-management; and a good business mind in order to be able to effectively manage remuneration from clients, deadlines to be met, and a consistently high level of professionalism.

While not everyone who manages to become a successful freelance translator has had a formal education, nowadays it would be unusual not to have obtained at least a primary degree before going down this route. There are an ever-increasing number of translation degrees being offered in third level institutions, many of which specialize in particular areas of translation (medical, legal, technical, and so on) at some point. It is essential to thoroughly research these courses to ascertain which ones turn out graduates who actually end up working in the industry as opposed to possessing an expensive but useless piece of paper. Freelance translators more regularly gain their primary degree in a particular field of study, and afterwards take a postgraduate course in translation studies.

Initially, finding work can be incredibly difficult. In most cases, when launching a career in translation you'll need to be doing something else part time to support yourself until you become established. The rates charged at the outset will probably need to be very low in order for a client to take you on with your lack of experience – something they're generally very reluctant to do. It is often necessary and worthwhile to do some small jobs for free so as to prove your abilities and be given an opportunity. Although translation agencies (the primary means of getting work as a freelancer) will usually refuse to hire you without several years of experience behind you – a catch 22 considering you often can't get work without them hiring you – some of them do offer traineeships. These will be very badly paid, if not entirely voluntary.

Bear in mind that doing this kind of thing will usually produce results and at the very least gain you contacts in the industry, and networking is vital in this job. There are online agencies such as www.proz.com and www.translatorscafe.com where potential clients can find your profile, and which provide helpful support networks for translators as well as advertising job offers. If, like me, you are only interested in literary translation, the British Council website (www.britishcouncil.org) offers valuable information along with providing many helpful links.

While going freelance is hugely unpredictable and requires a lot more work than you'll get paid for in the early stages, most translators who opt for this type of career do so because they are attracted to working from home, managing their time to suit their lifestyle, and not being answerable to anyone. ⟩

Freelance indexer

Liz Lemal is a freelance indexer, copy editor, and proofreader, and also offers word processing services. Her clients include mainstream publishers and individual authors, students, and design companies. She can be contacted through her website www.writeideauk.com.

⟨ Many people presume that the index comes automatically with the book, not realizing that it is compiled separately, usually by someone other than the author – the indexer. It is a specialist skill to be able to pick out of the text specific terms and meanings and convert them into headings that the reader is likely to look under. Therefore, it is vital that you have an excellent knowledge of, and are comfortable with, the subject you are indexing. As well as back-of-the-book indexing, there is a wide variety of other fields that require indexing, including databases, medical records, family histories, and audio-visual collections.

With no educational qualifications apart from GCEs and no publishing experience or contacts, I knew it would be harder to prove myself competent in the publishing world, even though my spelling and grammar were excellent and I loved reading. My first step, and one I recommend to any aspiring indexer, was to join the Society of Indexers. They have an excellent accreditation course (I also did a proofreading course and a copy-editing course; anything to increase my knowledge of the editorial world). The Society of Indexers has an online forum, which I also found very helpful in getting to know more about the indexing world.

Publishing is a hard industry to get into, easier if you are qualified in certain subjects so you can target relevant publishers/companies. If you don't have publishing experience or contacts, then it can be a case of cold calling as many people as you can and hope you're lucky. Continual professional development is important. Also keep up to date with relevant technology. Networking is important and I recommend LinkedIn for finding contacts and getting to know people.

If you're a sociable animal, then freelancing might not be for you. Self-discipline is necessary to avoid distraction – the 10-minute break that turns into 30, the phone call that could have waited till after work. But to me, the freedom I have to work when I want is what it's all about. I am my own boss – and I love it! '

SUMMARY

✓ Freelancing gives you the freedom of transition into different roles and broadening your skillset.

✓ Do your research: go to seminars, do some courses, and talk to other professionals in the field you want to move into and become an expert yourself.

✓ Offer new services as an addition to your existing ones, at least until your new line of business has taken off.

✓ Be careful about adopting too many specialist areas at once; you might find that you're juggling more than you can cope with!

✓ Promote and market your new service to your existing clients and fellow freelancers, so they can help spread the word.

✓ Be courageous, determined, and confident about the scope of your abilities and never underestimate your talent!

10
INSPIRATIONAL STORIES

Making the decision to become a freelancer is truly a leap of faith: faith in your own abilities; faith that you will get work (even when it seems like you will never work again!); and faith that you can succeed. There are plenty of occasions when we've experienced the 'wobbles' about our career choices, but thankfully, words of wisdom from other experts in the field have helped to put us back on the right track.

Publishing covers such a broad range of roles for freelancers, so we have sought out some experienced folk from across the spectrum to provide you with their stories and experiences in publishing. We hope you find them as inspirational as we have and that this chapter helps you to keep the faith.

A JOURNEY THROUGH PUBLISHING

Tom Hardy has worked in publishing for over 30 years, both freelance and in-house. He currently works in-house for Pearson Education as an international publisher for maths and sciences. His role involves commissioning new titles, implementing new publishing programmes and initiatives, and collaborating with overseas publishers.

❛When I look back at how I ended up in publishing, I realize I probably didn't go about it in the most conventional way. Before starting university, I had spent my gap year in East Africa and it gave me the travel bug. So, when I finished my degree in Natural Sciences (Biochemistry and Physiology) I was determined to find a way to travel as long as somebody else covered the cost! Thanks to joining the VSO programme as a volunteer, I spent a couple of years teaching in Nigeria, which subsequently led to another teaching post in the Caribbean, where I spent a further three years before personal circumstances persuaded me – albeit reluctantly – to head home to the UK.

As I was adjusting to the vagaries of the English weather once more, I wondered what on earth I was going to do with my life. Much as I loved teaching, I felt like taking my career in a new direction, but had no idea where I could apply my skills. After much soul-searching (and frantically circling the ads in the job section of the local newspaper) I came across a vacancy with an educational publisher as a maths and sciences editor in their Africa and Caribbean division, which sounded perfect. Unfortunately, I didn't get the job, but it gave me an interest in publishing and so I decided to wait until the next opportunity came up.

Eventually, I got a job as a junior editor at Cambridge University Press within their schools division where I stayed for seven years. I then worked with Macmillan for four years. Due to shifting changes and takeovers within the industry, I was made redundant and for the first time experienced what it was like to be a full time freelancer. Although it was not my choice to work freelance, looking back, it was the right thing to do. I had become a bit fed up with all the politics involved in the publishing world at the time and felt I would be better off being my own boss for a while. Besides, I wanted to create a business based on my own skills rather than worrying about the impact on my role should my employer go through another takeover or re-organization. Usually freelancing is associated with uncertainty but, at the time, it seemed far more secure than working in house!

Fortunately, I had a fair bit of experience behind me, a decent track record, a respectable reputation and a good network of contacts within the industry, so freelancing wasn't as daunting as it could have been. After I had been freelancing for a year, I was asked by Macmillan to work for them in-house for three days a week, as a commissioning editor for science and maths for their African markets. This meant that I still had two days a week to work as freelancer for other clients. Much as I had been enjoying the freelance life, I must admit that it was a relief to be employed by Macmillan for those three days, because at least I knew that whatever happened, I would have that pay cheque delivered to me every month. It also made me part of the company and gave me the power to initiate projects and make real changes, a luxury not always available to a freelancer. It really was the best of both worlds.

After a few months, I was asked to join Macmillan full-time – but I turned them down. I wanted to remain freelance so I could work for other clients – the variety of work and flexibility of lifestyle was very important to me. Those two days were also precious to me as I was able to get involved in different types of work such as teaching courses at the Publishing Training Centre. I probably wouldn't have had these sort of opportunities had I agreed to work for Macmillan full-time.

However, gradually, the volume of work that I was doing for Macmillan started to spill over into those precious two freelance days, and I ended up spending more and more time on Macmillan projects. In the end, I joined Macmillan full time, and gave up my freelance life for another ten years. However, fate stepped in once more, and I ended up back freelancing again for another three years. Very recently, I was offered a full-time role with Pearson

Education, again, working in their international section that was too interesting to turn down. So, now I find myself back in the world of full-time employment.

My freelance life has had its fair share of ups and downs, and I do miss my life as a freelancer and the freedom it entails. I haven't the time to do simple things any more, like paying bills or even getting my hair cut! Daily tasks I would normally fit into my flexible weekly schedule are a thing of the past. Fortunately, I live near Pearson so I don't have to worry about the added expense or hassle of commuting. It would have been quite a shock to go from working from home to squeezing onto a train at rush hour.

I remember one publisher told me she was happy to give me work because I was "a safe pair of hands". This is exactly how you want publishers to see you – as someone who can deliver; in other words that their project is going to be in safe hands. I know a number of freelancers who will only work for a limited number of publishers because they have built up such a good relationship with them. After all, it is difficult to build up 50 different relationships of equal merit; sometimes it's better to have a strong, long-lasting relationship with a few publishers rather than doing ad hoc work here and there for publishers that don't pay as well or that micro-manage you or don't take your suggestions into account and so on.

I find working in-house more demanding, especially as my role involves quite a bit of travel which can, sometimes, eat into the weekends. However, it is also great to work within a team and see projects through to fruition. I feel more effective as part of a company team, even though it means giving up flexibility, freedom, the peace of working in your own, and those precious lie ins!

On the other hand, I feel I achieved more when I was working at home – working in-house means dealing with endless emails, constant meetings, phone calls, chatting to other people (I work in a very friendly office), and many other distractions. Of course working from home has its own interruptions and it can be tempting to get too involved with household stuff, like getting the wardrobe fitters in or even doing a full-blown refurbishment!

Freelancing within publishing is a wonderfully versatile career. From graduates to career-changers to retirees, there is plenty of work available at all levels. There are excellent training courses out there that include distance learning, and cater for all levels. My advice to those who are looking to get into freelance publishing is to try and get some work experience with a publisher either through a short internship during the summer holidays (if you're a student), or working in-house for a couple of years. This will help to establish a good network of contacts and build up a good reputation. You will also learn where your skills lie and how you fit into the process. After all, one of the best ways to learn about a profession is to be in it. '

THE ACCIDENTAL FREELANCER

Victoria Hunt has worked in publishing since 2004. After working for in-house editorial departments at Random House and Orion, she completed a postgrad diploma in magazine journalism and moved to trade magazine *Publishing News*. When that folded in 2008, she worked as a freelance journalist and editor for a year before returning to a full-time role as a sub-editor on a national health website. Her blog is www.victoriahunt.wordpress.com.

‘In the summer of 2008 I was made redundant after the trade magazine I worked for folded. It was hard enough for me who had been there only a year and loved my eclectic role; those who had been there for more than two decades were devastated. Coming as it did on the eve of a recession, recruitment agencies had none of the opportunities they would have had a few years earlier, as it became apparent that every company in the industry was either shedding staff or experiencing a recruitment freeze.

I never intended to become a freelancer, but as it was to be a year before I started my current full-time position (as a sub-editor on a website), and with a mortgage to pay, I couldn't just up sticks and go travelling. But I didn't know where to begin either. My editorial skillset was varied; I was 26 years old with two-and-a-half years of administrative and some editorial experience in trade publishing, and, following a postgrad diploma, a year's experience in magazine journalism, where I had written news and features, covered industry events, and project managed spin-off publications. It was my dream job, but it no longer existed. I powered off passionate applications to rival magazines for junior reporter roles but it seemed they wanted new graduates whom they could pay less and mould into their own style. I couldn't really complain, having once benefited from these hiring policies myself!

In the end, and to my grateful surprise, friends came to my rescue. Having let people know of my plight only in the expectation of being invited out to drown my sorrows, I was amazed and touched when an old university friend emailed to say that his bandmate was working part-time for a newspaper that needed some cover in their production department; was I interested? That enquiry led to five months of regular work in a busy office laying out pages in Quark (which added a professional string to my bow) and writing book reviews, which only ended when someone came back from maternity leave.

This was followed by another stroke of luck, as yet another university friend, himself a journalist, told me over a drink that he knew someone working for a publishing company that produced glossy customer magazines for upmarket luxury brands. She was looking for a freelance sub-editor to take on contract work, and with my newly acquired Quark skills I got several months' work there too. But perhaps inevitably given the financial crisis, the market for private jets and yachts evaporated overnight and the company went into administration, which meant that many of its creditors, including me, didn't get paid towards the end. It could have been disastrous for my bank balance, but by that point I'd been offered my current job – although ironically (naively?) I had put off starting so that I could "honour my commitment" to the magazine publisher, so it felt like a double loss in earnings.

As enjoyable and varied as freelancing had been – and by this time I had picked up feature commissions and news shifts on other publications, mainly through former work contacts – the financial precariousness weighed me down and it was with relief that I returned to a payroll. I still write the odd freelance article, but I no longer have to rely on the income it generates. But it was a very useful experience that has made me feel much more confident about the idea of returning to freelancing in the future, perhaps when juggling a family.

What did I learn? First of all, the friendships you make at university are of more importance than I could ever have realized, and are absolutely worth hanging on to and nurturing. This may sound obvious, but one of the friends who helped me had, in our first year, broken my heart quite spectacularly, and at that point I nearly resolved to have nothing more to do with him. Keeping him in my life as a friend, however painful at the time and however much I questioned my sanity, ultimately rewarded me in more ways than one.

I also, more prosaically, learnt a lot about the value and integrity of money. When I was working for the newspaper, I was paid weekly after invoicing for my hours. Looking back I realize how generous and helpful this was, but at the time I didn't appreciate it, particularly as, at nine pounds an hour for four days a week in a ramshackle, freezing East London office, I felt underpaid. I complained a few times and towards the end I did get a rise.

But imagine my delight then, when I moved to the luxury magazine publisher and for the first job was offered £600 for five days' work in swanky offices near Sloane Square. The thrill faded when I discovered it was payable "30 days after publication" and publication date was at least two months away. It took more than four months of repeated chasing and refusal to commit to any more work before I received the money. I should have realized that the company was in trouble, but I continued accepting work and even managed to insist that for future projects I was paid in monthly instalments, which at first I was. But when it eventually went into administration I was left almost £1,000 out of pocket. All that glittered was certainly not gold.

Finally, I came to the realization that in my eagerness to get back onto a payroll, with every free day (of which there were many) spent desperately scanning online vacancies and pulling together applications, I wasn't giving the freelancing my best shot; it was job-hunting's poor relation. As a result, I wasn't selling myself nearly as hard as I should have been. If I had my time again, I'd have my own website set up in no time, adorned with electronic portfolio (rather than in a black case currently gathering dust under my bed) and contact details, to be circulated far and wide. I'd accept all offers to be listed in directories, I'd have business cards made, I'd go to media networking events, and I'd network much harder at other events. That's how it's done, you see. A freelance friend of mine came to my last birthday party where she was introduced to someone else I know who works for a charity. Within a month she had a published interview on their work in a double-page spread for a national tabloid. *That* was no accident. '

CALLING ALL FREELANCERS!

Katie Kirk is the director of Freelancers in the UK (www.free lancersintheuk.co.uk), an online careers site that aims to bring together freelance professionals based all over the UK, raise their profiles, and showcase their skills and services to a global audience, without the need for a personal website. Katie can be contacted at katie@freelancers intheuk.co.uk.

'I've always wanted to work in publishing but got there in a roundabout route, like many people, via a degree in languages, a stint in university administration, and six months as brochure executive with Page & Moy! I had studied part-time for a diploma in editorial skills but it was a fortuitous move to Loughborough and a speculative application to Ladybird Books resulting in a role as publicity assistant that marked the beginning of my publishing career and one of the happiest times of my life. I was able to attend exhibitions, arrange competitions, have regular contact with schools, nurseries, and children, give out prizes, do radio interviews, write press releases and advertorials...working with such a fantastic product and some very inspirational people. At the time, flexible working wasn't as prevalent as now and many of my colleagues worked full-time, and then some. I left Ladybird Books to have a baby and had then planned to return part-time as assistant brand manager, but in the interim the company closed its factory in Loughborough and relocated to London, leaving a rather big dent in the local area.

The decision to work freelance was made after a few years of administrative work in the Civil Service and precipitated by an appendectomy! Many people have told me that a life-changing event has been the catalyst for taking the plunge to work freelance and I'm no exception. The benefits that a freelance lifestyle can bring are well-documented – the flexibility to juggle domestic commitments and childcare, and certainly as a mother, I have been able to fit in work around nursery, school, extra-curricular clubs, and so on. But it also means that you need to have total focus during the times that you do work and to exercise discipline to make sure deadlines are met, new leads are followed up, and administration isn't sidelined. And of course it's a question of feast or famine, financially. My advice is to share your life (and bank account!) with someone whose income is reliable, whose hours are predictable and who is happy for you to be the flexible one! It's a very powerful lifestyle choice... many friends of mine say that the switch to permanent work is a step too far for them, and I'm inclined to agree.

In the summer of 2004 I was contacted by a prospective client, James, who wanted me to work on a freelance copywriting project. I was overcommitted at the time and couldn't help, but the conversation drifted naturally on to how difficult he as a client had found it to source someone local for an editorial project. I agreed.

His business instinct kicked in and my creative juices started flowing ... in that ten-minute conversation we sowed the seeds for a careers website for freelancers. I had the overwhelming sense that we could create a useful, viable resource. It was a champagne moment!

So, with James as my co-director, I decided to use my knowledge, connections, and contacts to build a central register of freelance professionals in the UK. What I didn't take into account was the genuine business need to have a searchable register exclusively for UK-based freelance professionals in a wide range of sectors, not just publishing. Clients cited this as one of the most frustrating aspects of sourcing freelance help – and were quick to feed back very positively. Membership grew at an astonishing rate.

Freelancers in the UK is essentially a register of UK based-freelancers that is searchable by geographical location, skillset, and name, giving members high-profile exposure without the need for a personal website and providing a platform for members to access projects and contracts posted by external agencies and organizations. It caters as much for individuals with an enthusiastic hobby in Middle England as high-flying journalists for the broadsheets in London and IT contractors in Glasgow, and everyone in between!

In terms of time and energy, the business was extremely expensive. It was a labour of love, blood, sweat, and tears. When we first started the website in 2005, James and I skill swapped: his software, my words; his expertise with search engine optimization, my network of contacts in the editorial field; his boyish sense of humour, my irony. It's difficult to put a cost on this. I guess the most realistic way of representing our investment is that I turned down paid work to build the site over a few months and James invested his experience, his staff, and his software, so for me it's measurable in lost earnings...thousands!

James and I worked as a team with a little background support. We covered all functions between us until October 2009 when I became sole director of the site to allow James to pursue other interests. I'm supported now by a network of people offering accountancy, marketing advice, and technical input, and find that this works really well. Although I often wish I could clone myself...

Although running Freelancers in the UK takes up most of my time, I still manage to work as a freelance copywriter, proofreader, and editor, and enjoy the diversity of both roles. For me, working from home is not only practical but desirable. I can flex to suit domestic circumstances (and accommodate two small people who live with me), I find that I'm more motivated, and I actively enjoy the freedom to plan my day and my week. I'm lucky enough to have a good network of friends, including some who also work from home, so I get my social fix. Alas, the housekeeping suffers.

I work almost 200 hours a week – at least that's what it feels like! I work a long week on a split shift to accommodate domestic commitments and I also work weekends. The website generates enquiries on a daily basis and there is administrative and planning work to do. I wouldn't swap it for the world. It's so very empowering to take a business concept and make it work.

Although the temptation can be to work round the clock, intellectually I know this is Not A Good Idea and doesn't favour a healthy work/life balance, which is what freelancing is supposed to facilitate. Contrary to popular belief, I recommend retaining some fluidity – don't fix or define the day too formally. It's about taking advantage of opportunities that sometimes can't be timetabled. I can honestly say that I've never been tempted to play hooky and down tools – that comes from doing a job you love.

Money's a great facilitator but personally, enjoying what I do and being recognized for having achieved something that is useful and creative ticks my boxes. This is how I would measure success in my late thirties. Ten years ago, making money would have seemed more important. And anyway, time is the new money!

The greatest challenge to starting up a business is juggling the amount of time needed to devote to a new enterprise with other demands and responsibilities, whether these are domestic, professional, or personal. There are no rule books and it can sometimes be very hard to know when to draw the line: the temptation is to throw yourself whole-heartedly into the new venture. Starting five years earlier would have been a good move. Ah, the joy of retrospect . . .

As we emerge from recession and start to gain confidence again, I'm committed to building and refining the website, expanding the number of categories we have to reflect the move towards flexible working and freelancing throughout the UK and across all business sectors. My immediate goal is to attract more organizations, agencies, and businesses to take advantage of the very wide range of skills and services our members provide.

So here's my advice for all you budding entrepreneurs out there: don't be afraid to follow your instinct and your interest – this isn't a dress rehearsal. If I'd known at 21 what I know now, I'd have saved myself 15 years of going through the motions to some extent. We're shaped so easily in our youth, by what others expect of us and propel us toward.

You need to be tenacious to the point of sheer bloody-mindedness, particularly if you're a woman: motivated, dedicated, realistic, and yet optimistic. You need to have belief in yourself, the product or service, and a very thick skin because it's a given that you'll encounter resistance and even jealousy along the way.

I believe that a lot of business instinct comes from inside, it's almost a personality trait, but there isn't much substitution for sheer graft; as Thomas Edison said, "Opportunity is missed by most people because it is dressed in overalls and looks like work." '

IS IT CATCHING? VIRAL AND DIGITAL MARKETING IN THE BOOK WORLD

Lorelei Mathias is the author of *Lost for Words* and *Step On It, Cupid*, and is currently a copywriter at ad agency Glue, while working on her third novel (and trying not to distract herself with ways to promote it). You can see her virals at Youtube.com/amelieholden or Myspace.com/steponitcupid. Her novel writing website is Loreleimathias.com. And her advertising work is at Lollyandnat.com. She also writes a blog for ad industry mag Campaignlive.co.uk.

> ' *"And we'll need a huge publicity blitz. Full review coverage . . . and anything out of the ordinary we can think of. Stunts. Ambience. Dressing up. We really need to push the boat out with this one . . . Oh, and what are those things called – viruses?"* *

Of course, Belinda (head of fiction in my fictional publishing house) means virals. In her own dippy way though, she's onto something. Viral marketing of books isn't something new or tremendously tricky to do. However, it does bring with it the possibility of reaching new and different kinds of readers. And it enables authors to get involved with the marketing of their own books. Which I think is a great thing.

The trouble is, "viral" is a misnomer. You can't insist something you create is "viral", just by calling it that. All you can hope is that the idea – whether it's a website, email, or book trailer – is interesting enough that people will pass it on.

Before I was lucky enough to be published, I spent over four years working at Random House as an in-house creative. Everything from big budget "Nothing Grips like Grisham" campaigns with giant books stuck to billboards to small budget "Super Good Day" stunts with red Beetles, for Mark Haddon's *Curious Incident.* One thing which was very clear from doing that job was just how very crowded the market is. It didn't take me long to realize that to make a book stand out these days, you really do have to think of something special.

When my first book was published in 2006, I knew my publisher (LBD)'s marketing would be brand- not author-led. But being an ad creative, I couldn't help thinking of ideas to support it (an occupational hazard). So when my book was picked out for a Waterstone's January sale, I couldn't help wanting to do something to help it along – without treading on toes of course. So I ended up writing a TV script to use online. We couldn't afford to run a TV ad – but I could afford to write one, and then use the internet to send it on its journey via YouTube. At the time YouTube was a pretty much untapped area for book marketing. Back then the idea of a book trailer didn't really exist – but it's now almost common vernacular.

Anyway, once I'd written the script, I sent it to the actress Sarah Smart (from *Wallander*) whom I'm a big fan of. She loved the script and she very kindly gave her time for the project. (In my dreams, we would both love for her to play the part of Amelie if there was ever a feature film made of it.)

Many favours later, I managed to get the film produced on a shoestring and put it onto YouTube. Once the YouTube trailer and the blog had been organically seeded across chatrooms and friends' inboxes, things took off. The viral had thousands of hits, and spread to hundreds of sites and blogs around the globe; everywhere from Croatia to China. It's also led to encouraging PR. One review began, "after seeing the trailer for *Step On It, Cupid*, I just had to give it a read".

I also created a fictitious profile on MySpace for Amelie, the novel's heroine, and a blog for her as "the world's most reluctant speed-dater". This was the perfect way for Amelie to spew out all her different neuroses and generally have a rant, and it was a great way to publicize samples of the book. By creating the online identity of Amelie, the world's most reluctant speed-dater, I was then able to dot her around all the networks and dating chatrooms, so that people clicked on her out of curiosity and were led to the book by her ad-that-didn't-look-like-an-ad. The response was brilliant, with hundreds of new invitations from "friends" for Amelie, and comments being added to the blog from other speed-daters.

I was fortunate to win Campaign of the Quarter from the Book Marketing Society, which led to a lot more spin off PR in *Publishing News* and *The Bookseller* and a talk at the London Book Fair. And, bizarrely, there are comments on blogs calling it "the best book trailer for a book ever!", which is kind!

Oh and there was also a spike in my Amazon sales ranking. But that said, I don't believe the value in a "viral" lies directly in sales – it's more about generating awareness, talkability, and that old elixir of publishing: word of mouth.

These days, simply shoving a quote on the book jacket and reproducing it to four-times-sheet dimensions isn't going to make enough impact. And while it's common practice for a Tube campaign to be binned after two weeks, a YouTube or MySpace page costs nothing in media space and has no time limit. I started this campaign back in 2006, and while it isn't fresh any more, it's still live, four years on. It's still being viewed by someone in the world every day. This sort of campaign really is the most direct, cost-effective way for your fictional characters to mingle with your target audience – wherever they are in the world. A poster on the Tube can't bring your character to life as vividly as a fluffy pink profile on a real social network, or a short film that dramatizes their predicament in a compelling way.

The really wonderful thing about these brave new marketing methods is that they're all accessible to the author. In some ways, MySpace, YouTube *et al.* have really made things more democratic, have levelled the playing field for those with small budgets and big ideas. In an article I wrote for *The Bookseller* back in 2007, I wondered aloud whether, to some extent, power was shifting away from the marketing meeting (like the typical one above in *Lost for Words),* and into the hands of the author, the bloggers, and the networkers.

Four years on, I'd say this is truer than ever. The only difference is that there are now infinitely more online tools to add to the mix.

Facebook was in its infancy when I did my viral campaign, but today, there are also Twitter, iPhone Apps, and all kinds of new-fangled technology that offer yet more power to the author. I can barely keep up with them all! At the moment, I have all my films hosted on my author site, Loreleimathias.com, and I have lots of ideas on how to expand it out. I write a blog for the advertising industry on Campaignlive.co.uk, but any more distractions than that and it's impossible to find time to actually do the writing itself! I'm writing my third book at the moment and I have to exercise some restraint sometimes – I can't help coming up with viral ideas while I'm writing it!

So, any author thinking of dabbling in self-marketing should be careful of that – it can become addictive . . . '

* Extract from *Lost for Words* (Headline Books, July 2007)

IF AT FIRST YOU DON'T SUCCEED . . .

Spencer Honniball is a freelance writer from London. Since the publication of his first book, *Beg, Steal or Borrow*, an authorized biography of Babyshambles, he has been involved in various ghostwriting and screenwriting projects. His website is www.spencer honniball.com.

'Thinking of becoming a freelance writer? My advice – go for it. If you're confident enough in your command of language, and feel you're at a stage in your career where you'd like to work for yourself, then the potential rewards are fantastic. Self-motivation, coupled with a firm belief in your abilities, are, of course, essential; though the satisfaction of being your own boss is considerable, it is counterbalanced by the stress of bringing work in.

Like any other industry, much depends on how well-connected you are. Lacking an extensive list of contacts or not being in possession of great networking skills doesn't by any means spell failure, but joining societies, placing examples of your work as abundantly as possible, and meeting like-minded people can only benefit your cause.

Much like the business of writing in general, considerable amounts of time and effort may come to nothing, but lucky breaks, at least in my experience, are often the result of that overused cliché: "being in the right place at the right time"; creating your own luck, in a sense, because the more you put yourself out there, the greater the possibility of building relationships in a community that can be surprisingly warm and supportive to newcomers.

Most writers with even the most rudimentary knowledge of this tough industry will have faced the manifold frustrations that eagerly greet those endeavouring to make a living out of their use of words. Piranha-like agents, interminably long lapses in time between submission and response, and widespread indifference are just some of the many joys awaiting us, but the readiness with which help can be sought comes as considerable relief to those of a nervier disposition.

And while rejection is part and parcel of the freelancer's life, breakthroughs, when they arrive, are all the richer for them. As somebody still cutting their teeth as a full-time writer, I can't attest to long-term success, though it was only through perseverance that I got my breakthrough; and suspect that, if I am able to prolong my career, determination will have much to do with it.

Try not to be dissuaded by unhelpful criticism of your work, never lose faith in yourself and keep practising. Forgive me for stating the blindingly obvious, but the more time you spend harnessing your talent, the better your output. And the better the output, the more chance of getting recognized and enhancing your work prospects.

As mentioned already, great reserves of patience are likely to be required to reach the level you aspire to, and this can be hard to find if money is scarce and your prospects appear bleak. The people you require to green-light projects will most likely have little time to spare, causing tailbacks that can sometimes take months to shift, though once additional work has been secured, and your portfolio begins to swell, your marketability – a horrible word, I know, but one that you may well hear agents harp on about – will also benefit. This is why it's so important, at least if your career is in its infancy, to try and put your eggs in as many baskets as possible, so to speak, in the hope that one of those projects will come to fruition.

Unfortunately, the frustration won't end when the work starts coming in. Much of your energy will be spent firing off and responding to emails, detracting from time you would far sooner spend trying to meet deadlines on your current projects. You may encounter delays through no fault of your own, but try as always to keep your ultimate target in mind, and don't be discouraged from attempting to realize it.

Get a website put up on the net and post samples of your material there, explaining what sort of work you wish to invite. Try and find a good agent through whom you can submit your material, or make approaches yourself. If favouring the latter, submit to as many companies as possible, because the unpalatable truth is that some will ignore you altogether, with those who don't very probably taking longer than you'd like to respond. Ensure that your work is in the best possible shape as, for the most part, you'll get one shot per project. Take your time and give yourself the best possible chance of securing interest.

The life of the freelancer is not for the faint-hearted, though while the early stages might prove trying, the return can be wonderfully fulfilling. The key, as far as I can tell, is to keep striving for improvement, polishing your talent continually and never conceding defeat. There are so many interesting people with whom you can collaborate, and the manner of work sometimes so far removed from what you might have expected, that your journey will be far from dull. Good luck – and stick with it! "

USEFUL CONTACTS

BUSINESS SUPPORT

Business Link

A government-funded free business advice and support service.

Web: www.businesslink.gov.uk

Tel: 0845 600 9 006

Direct.gov.uk

The government's website containing loads of information on matters such as tax, benefits and employment.

Web: www.direct.gov.uk

HMRC

The tax authority provides help on taxation issues on its website and via its helpline.

Web: www.hmrc.gov.uk

Tel: various specialized helplines; check website for details.

Professional Contractors Group

Represents, supports, and promotes freelancers.

Web: www.pcg.org.uk

Email: admin@pcg.org.uk

Tel: 020 8897 9970

NETWORKING

BNI
Business networking organization with local chapters operating a shared referral system.
Web: www.bni-europe.com/uk
Email: bniuk@eurobni.com
Tel: 01923 891 999

Chamber of Commerce
You find these local business networking and support groups in towns and cities all over Britain. Search online for your local one, or take a look at the British Chambers of Commerce website.
Web: www.britishchambers.org.uk

Ecademy
A global online business networking site where you can set up a profile and market your services.
Web: www.ecademy.com
Email: info@britishchambers.org.uk

Everywoman.com
Online networking for women.
Web: www.everywoman.com
Tel: 020 7981 2574

Federation of Small Businesses
Offers local networking opportunities and business support.
Web: www.fsb.org.uk
Tel: 01253 336 000

LinkedIn
Offers a connections-based approach to online networking.
Web: www.linkedIn.com

Social networking
Sites you may use for connecting with clients and sharing news and business information.
Bebo: www.bebo.com
Facebook: www.facebook.com
MySpace: www.myspace.com
Twitter: www.twitter.com

Women in Business
Networking for women.
Web: www.wibn.co.uk
Email: enquiries@wibn.co.uk
Tel: 0845 004 9426

WORKING FROM HOME

Telework Association
Promotes home-working, provides information, and has a members' forum for chatting with others in the same boat.
Web: www.tca.org.uk
Tel: 0800 616008

SOCIETIES AND ORGANIZATIONS

Association of Illustrators
Supports and promotes illustrators.
Web: www.theaoi.com
info@theaoi.com
Tel: 020 7613 4328

Book Marketing Society
Networking, events, and resources for those involved in book marketing.

Web: www.bookmarketingsociety.co.uk

Diversity in Publishing
Network promoting diversity across the industry.
Web: www.dipnet.org.uk
Tel: 020 8875 4824

The Galley Club
Social organization for those working in publishing that holds regular events.
Web: www.galleyclub.co.uk

National Union of Journalists (NUJ)
Union for journalists and other editorial workers in Britain and Ireland.
Web: www.nuj.org.uk
Email: info@nuj.org.uk

Oxford Publishing Society
Hosts Oxford-based publishing events.
Web: http://opusnet.co.uk

Picture Research Association
Courses, information, listings, and resources for picture researchers.
Web: www.picture-research.org.uk

Publishers Publicity Circle
Meetings and job ads for book publicists.
www.publisherspublicitycircle.co.uk

Publishing Scotland
Body representing the Scottish publishing industry, open to membership by publishers and individuals working in the industry.
Web: www.publishingscotland.co.uk
Email: enquiries@publishingscotland.org

Tel: 0131 228 6866

Society of Authors
Meetings, events, promotional opportunities, and support for authors.
Has groups for book illustrators and translators.
Web: www.societyofauthors.org
Tel: 020 7373 6642

Society for Editors and Proofreaders
Offers resources, training, mentoring, and accreditation.
Web: www.sfep.org.uk
Email: administration@sfep.org.uk
Tel: 020 8785 5617

Society of Indexers
Represents book indexers, offering training, information, local groups,
publications, and promotion opportunities.
Web: www.indexers.org.uk
Email: info@indexers.org.uk
Tel: 0845 872 6807

Society of Young Publishers
Offers events and resources (including job bulletins) for anyone
working in publishing. Branches in London and Oxford.
Web: www.thesyp.org.uk

Society of Women Writers and Journalists
Networking and support for female writers.
Web: www.swwj.co.uk

Women in Publishing
Networking and support for women working in the industry.
Web: www.wipub.org.uk

Email: info@wipub.org.uk

Writers' Guild of Great Britain
Trade union for writers.
Web: www.writersguild.org.uk
Tel: 020 7833 0777

BOOK FAIRS

Frankfurt Book Fair
World's largest trade fair, usually held in October.
Web: www.frankfurt-book-fair.com

London Book Fair
An excellent networking opportunity, usually held in April.
Web: www.londonbookfair.co.uk

PUBLISHING TRAINING COURSES

Editorial Training
Proofreading, editing, and writing courses.
Web: www.edittrain.co.uk
Email: info@edittrain.co.uk
Tel: 0845 0171 059

Imago
Offers training in book production, design, and rights.
Web: www.imago.co.uk
Email: sales@imago.co.uk
Tel: 01844 337000

The Publishing Training Centre
Courses on all aspects of publishing, from editorial to project management, software to copyright.

Web: www.train4publishing.co.uk
Email: publishing.training@bookhouse.co.uk
Tel: 020 8874 2718

Postgraduate publishing course providers
City University (London): www.city.ac.uk
Kingston University (London): www.kingston.ac.uk
London College of Communication: www.lcc.arts.ac.uk
UCL (London): www.publishing.ucl.ac.uk
Napier University (Edinburgh): www.napier.ac.uk
Oxford Brookes University: www.ah.brookes.ac.uk
University of Central Lancashire: www.uclan.ac.uk
University of Plymouth: www.plymouth.ac.uk
University of Stirling: www.external.stir.ac.uk

INDUSTRY PUBLICATIONS

Writers' and Artists' Yearbook
A book with accompanying site that provides advice and includes a full range of publishing resources.
Web: www.writersandartists.co.uk

The Bookseller
Magazine and website with the latest news, discussion, and jobs in publishing.
Web: www.thebookseller.com

Publishers Weekly
US-based site/mag that features global publishing news and jobs.
Web: www.publishersweekly.com

MARKETING RESOURCES

Freelancers in the UK

Website promoting freelancers and offering services of interest.
Web: www.freelancersintheuk.co.uk

Foliostop

Website designers for those working in the arts.
Web: www.foliostop.com

INDEX